ONE WEEK LOAN

The New Strategic Landscape

The New Strategic Landscape

Innovative Perspectives on Strategy

Julie Verity

First published 2012 by
PALGRAVE MACMILLAN

Palgrave Macmillan in the UK is an imprint of Macmillan Publishers Limited, registered in England, company number 785998, of Houndmills, Basingstoke, Hampshire RG21 6XS.

Palgrave Macmillan in the US is a division of St Martin's Press LLC, 175 Fifth Avenue, New York, NY 10010.

Palgrave Macmillan is the global academic imprint of the above companies and has companies and representatives throughout the world.

Palgrave® and Macmillan® are registered trademarks in the United States, the United Kingdom, Europe and other countries.

ISBN 978–0–230–35837–9

This book is printed on paper suitable for recycling and made from fully managed and sustained forest sources. Logging, pulping and manufacturing processes are expected to conform to the environmental regulations of the country of origin.

A catalogue record for this book is available from the British Library.

A catalog record for this book is available from the Library of Congress.

10 9 8 7 6 5 4 3 2 1
21 20 19 18 17 16 15 14 13 12

Printed and bound in Great Britain by
CPI Antony Rowe, Chippenham and Eastbourne

Contents

Figures and Table

Figures

Table

Acknowledgements

This book came about because of the encouragement from two colleagues, Robert Davies and Jeremy Kourdi, and the inspiration of working on strategy topics with the executive MBA students at Cass Business School.

I have been supported throughout by Robert, Janis and Mike.

Contributors joined the fray with enthusiasm and have been great people to work with. Thanks to all.

Contributors

Katie Best, PhD, is Foundation for Management Education Fellow at the London School of Economics, UK, as well as a freelance educator and consultant. She focuses on issues relating to work practice and communication in a range of workplaces, including higher education, the cultural sector and technology-rich environments.

Jean Boulton, PhD, MBA, MPhil, is a consultant and part-time academic, holding visiting academic positions at Cranfield School of Management, Bristol Business School and the University of Bath, in the UK. She is Director of Claremont Management Consultants Ltd, specialising in strategy and organisation development.

Bill Critchley, MBA, MSc, Clinical Diploma in Psychotherapy, Diploma in Organisational Consulting, practises as an organisation consultant, an executive coach and psychotherapist. He is Founder of the Ashridge Business School's Master's in Organisation Consulting and Joint Founder of the Ashridge Professional Doctorate in Organisation Consulting in the UK. He is also Founder and Director of the Ashridge Coaching for Organisation Consultants programme.

Robert Davies, PhD, MBA, FCII, provides advisory and educational services to a range of organisations in the fields of organisational change, global foresight, scenario planning, strategy development and innovation. He is a senior visiting fellow at Cass Business School, UK.

Gill Ereaut, MA FMRS FRSA, founded the consultancy Linguistic Landscapes in 2002, pioneering the application of methods developed from linguistics and discourse analysis to real and persistent organisational issues. Her work connects organisational culture and culture change with corporate, operational and brand strategy.

Kevin McCullagh founded Plan, following a background in design, marketing, engineering and academia. While at Plan and previously as Director of Foresight at the design consultancy Seymour Powell, he has offered consultancy services to design, marketing and corporate strategy departments of global brands. Kevin writes, speaks and broadcasts on design, technology and society.

Lewis Pinault has 20 years of consulting experience in improving organisational performance through people. He has designed and led transformation work in Europe, the United States and throughout Asia. He is the author of two books, *The Play Zone: Unlock Your Creative Genius and Connect with Consumers and Consulting Demons: Inside the Unscrupulous World of Global Corporate Consulting,* which was named one of *Fortune Magazine's* Best Business Books.

1
Introduction

Julie Verity

Each chapter in this book describes a different and relatively new way to conceptualise and appreciate strategy. It is written by an eclectic group of people who share expertise in strategy, but are from diverse backgrounds representing a matrix of disciplines, academia, practice and consultancy. It is about how we make sense of strategy from our experiences and through applying our theoretical training. From these diverse perspectives come shared themes and common insights that, we think, debunk some persistent but dated notions, bring strategy to life, make it real and are the future of effective strategic practice.

The philosophy

More than 20 years ago when I started studying strategy formally, I asked two professors of the subject the same question: *what is strategy?* Each gave radically different answers. One said that it was straightforward and about learning several matrices, rules and concepts; the other said that it was messy and complicated and that it would be years before I would have a good grasp on it. The first professor was schooled in economics, the traditional background for strategy academics. The other had studied anthropology. And that probably sums up the reasons for their answers. I concluded 20 years ago that the answer to my question was – *it depends* on how you think. Even after all this time, working on the cusp between strategy practice and academia, I think this is still a valid conclusion.

In the classroom, at the juncture when I have to explain this conclusion to MBA hopefuls I 'reach for' my father as an example. The poor man has been used as a stereotype in many of my lectures, because he is the archetypical planner. Brilliant at mathematics, an engineer and a lifer with the General Electric Company (GEC), where Arnold Weinstock ruled as CE (chief executive) for a significant period overlapping with the time my father worked there, he was trained within a 'hard' culture to see every challenge and objective as dependent on the plan which would deliver it. Once the plans were drawn and everything and everybody were in their places, lighting the touchpaper was all that was needed to set in motion the faultless path to success.

Of course, things did go wrong. But this was *not* a problem of the plan.

I often pondered why my father – a very intelligent man – didn't build plans that took account of the human capital involved. He could calculate and allow for tolerances in his engineering designs, knowing that steel would expand or shrink to *this* degree, under *these* conditions, but his plans took no account, nor included any tolerance for human behaviour. Every problem was approached in exactly the same way. Even when it came to family decisions: where should we go on holiday, how should we get there? Out would come the option-generation routine, then the decisions based on criteria such as the route with the least traffic (!), and finally the decision and the plan.

I make sense of how economics has influenced strategic thinking through this stereotype of my father, who would have delivered on time and to budget every time if only people didn't need to be involved. Economics has rules and these too have little tolerance for the quirks and idiosyncrasies of human beings. So, if you are schooled in strategy by an economist, strategy is about rules, and, as long as you follow the rules, strategy is relatively straightforward and easy. The organisation might not achieve the goal it set out to, but this is not because the rules are flawed.

This view of strategy is single-minded, straightforward, two-dimensional, mechanical and simple. Every problem can be tackled in the same way by using the same rules over and over again. Strategy is a plan (or a position – in the jargon), which is comforting because what to do next is known – it is in the plan.

The professor whose training was in anthropology looked through the organisational haze and didn't see the documents about strategy, and the numbers, plans or rules that guided them. Instead he focused on the people and how they behaved. What he saw was people coming together, having ideas, sharing, talking, deciding, doing, inventing, learning, telling stories, forming coalitions, having beliefs, acting on those beliefs, playing politics, resisting and retaliating, derailing and destroying. Wearing this 'anthropological' brand of eyeglasses reveals that what steers an organisation, in this direction or that, are the multiple thoughts and subsequent behaviours of people interacting with each other. In this reality, most people don't know about 'the' plan. They probably haven't seen that wonderful drawing on a huge sheet of paper, which (at least in my youthful days of doing holiday work in the drawing office at GEC) was tinged blue, felt warm when fresh from the printing machine and smelt heavenly. And if they had seen it, they probably wouldn't own it or understand it because they had no part in its creation. But they would look at it in awe and think how clever it was and, like me, love it for its certainty.

From my MBA classroom and executive learning suite experience, most people make sense of strategy by thinking of it as planning. As with all things human, however, there are the exceptions, there are those who stray towards the messy view. These people often work within exceptional organisational cultures; those often found in small companies which strive to sustain an entrepreneurial mindset, or in those organisations which have resisted centralised bureaucracy or a strong focus on profit maximisation, or they quite simply are freethinkers. But, even here, among the fleet-of-foot and truly differentiated, there is often an apologetic air about not having a strategic plan. A reason for this might be the combination of the number of books written about strategy plus what is taught in classrooms is strongly weighted towards the economist's view. So despite their success with their businesses or lives, these people feel bad that they are too busy to be doing what they *should* – that is making plans. They repeat that oft-used phrase: 'We are spending too much time **in** the business rather than **on** the business.'

While this weight of literature and brainwashing doubtless has an effect, there is also the influence of our own psychology. Just recently (April 2012), for example, I spent some time with a small company I have worked with off and on over the years. The leaders wanted to enter China and called for help with a strategy. At one point in the conversation, the CE said: 'We don't want the same experience as when we went to the USA. That was so messy and we made so many mistakes, this time we need a plan.' I tried to explain that the plan would not take all the pain away. There would still be mistakes, failures, trial and errors, and painful decisions to be made, but this didn't work. For the CE, the plan was a painkiller and all these concerns could be soothed away with a dose of planning, at least for the duration of the first steps taken into the unknown. On exactly the same day, I also met with an enlightened CFO who complained that his global organisation wanted to make five-year plans for the future when they had no idea how the recession would play out in Europe and the United States. He argued that the company should *not* do this because it was a waste of time and resources and that they would just be guessing most of the time. He did not win. The power of a plan to take the weight of responsibility for strategy is enormous.

So here lies the problem for the alternative theories and ideas about strategy that are 'out there' beyond economics and that are the subject of this book. These different ways of thinking are everything that is often considered unappealing, especially by those who are typically most successful in organisations, and therefore often have the strategy title. Hence the idea of strategy-as-plan is perpetuated. Messy strategy is not *always* organised, not *always* controllable, not simple or totally rational; it is often uncertain and doesn't always tell you *what will happen next.* It requires knowing about people, not just about numbers and the P&L or the tolerances of steel and the rules of economics. The crucial point with these alternative ways to think about strategy is that numbers, financials and economics are *secondary*, not primary. The ideas that are beyond economics make the unpredictable, difficult, emotional, complex and human strategic. In these approaches to strategy, the hardest tasks are elevated to be the strategists' responsibility.

Somewhere along the continuum, separating the professorial views described above, is how strategy happens in *your* mind, from *your* experience or what *you* want it to be.

If you are one of the many who experience strategy as a plan or as a framework that leads to a fairly certain outcome, reading this book might be unsettling and could be a struggle. But stick with it. Planning is valuable in some contexts but, we propose, not in all and not all the time. And so much has been written in this territory that the ideas can easily be found elsewhere. The perspectives this book invites you to explore, hold many exciting and valid ways to think about strategy and will give you a new, rich set of ideas to explore.

The ideas

Each chapter stands alone. Pick any one that sparks your interest as a place to start. For a taster and overview of common themes that emerge, read on.

Uncertainty and complexity

Chapters 2 and 3 are contributions from Jean Boulton and Robert Davies. These are placed together because both explore the big picture.

Jean's area of interest and study is complexity theory. In Chapter 2 – 'Strategy for a Complex World' – she introduces the ideas of the early 20th-century physicists, biologists and system thinkers, and makes these relevant to the current reality of business and organisations. She invites us to think about the world as a complex system – one that is open, interconnected, organic, contingent upon context and history, and one where the future is emergent.

Within complex systems, there are periods and areas of stability, where patterns and structures (of the business and/or landscape) persist for some time. Here, short-term planning and predictability are possible. But there are also instabilities, areas of turbulence and periods of great change. These can tip businesses and organisations into very different worlds, sometimes rapidly and dramatically. In a complex system, stability and emergence can happen together. Linearity and clear cause-and-effect linkages are *not* the rule; instead there are unintended consequences, spontaneity and surprises. Boundaries are hard to discern and luck is equally likely to deliver organisational success as are analysis, control and planning.

If we believe that our world is like a complex system, the managerial mindset that will be successful is the one that will be constantly updated with current information and open to experimentation and discovery. Therefore the recommendations are to take a portfolio approach, to promote diversity, to be adaptable and flexible, and to take the long and the short, the global and the local view *at the same time*. This means not being obsessed with dominance or being too strongly focused on one thing. This also means accepting that control is not always possible or desirable. As Jean explains, the complexity message is about balance and judgement.

One of the skills Jean recommends for coping with the uncertainty of a complex world is foresight and for this she recommends using scenario planning. Robert takes this topic to a new level in Chapter 3 – 'Strategy and the New Uncertainty' – by questioning if this 40-year-old technique is still relevant and sufficient for strategists today.

The focus for scenario thinking is uncertainty and how to make better strategic decisions while taking into account future uncertainty. Scenario thinking is probably the only long-standing strategy tool that takes uncertainty as its main focus. Its origins are in the military and influential think tanks of the Cold War era that served governments trying to make sense of the unpredictable behaviour of aggressive enemies. It is fundamentally a storytelling device which mixes imagination and rich information to create different plausible stories about the future. It promotes balanced thinking by using quantitative and qualitative information, rigorous analysis and creative imagination, plausible and possible thinking.

Robert argues that globalisation has changed our world significantly since the days of the Cold War and that there is an increased potential for 'catastrophic collapses' such as the 2007–08 credit crisis and the subsequent *Great Recession*. He suggests that this turbulent environment might be the new normal and if so uncertainty will be more important than ever as a focus of strategic thinking. He challenges that traditional scenario methodology is robust enough for this new reality, and finds that it has limitations.

Robert proposes a new approach called the Universal Thought Space. This lays out in advance the possible future worlds which will be determined by the motivations and behaviours of groups of people and the tensions between them, those which can be resolved and those which are irreconcilable. This focus on human behaviour is a key difference from earlier scenario techniques which were derived from exploring, selecting and combining a set of inanimate 'driving forces'.

Four powerful groups of actors with distinctive belief systems are the basis of the thought space. Robert suggests that the possible worlds within this thought space should be examined, discussed and rehearsed by the top management team as a way to free thinking about future possibilities and making better decisions for the long term.

Rebalanced minds

The need for balanced thinking is a common theme throughout the book and occurs as a major conclusion of Chapter 4 – 'Design Thinking'. This chapter was co-authored by Kevin McCullagh.

Chapter 4 seeks to explain the recent rise of interest in design and designers' minds, which apparently are balanced and view strategic problems in a unique way. The rise in popularity of design is probably, in part at least, due to the context of the new century, when growth from innovation is seen as an answer to the poor and declining performance of the established Western economies. Apple is also a living, in-your-face example of how design can work magic at the interface between technology and the consumer to deliver huge amounts of value. The fascination, therefore, is with the designers' skills, the art of crafting something completely new and desirable that has the potential to change the world by creating the sort of mania that Apple iPhone, iPods and iPads have stirred up everywhere.

The balance that designers are said to be able to keep in their minds is that between the analytic and the creative, the utilitarian and the aesthetically pleasing, and between the activities of the right and left brains. Design thinkers argue that business leaders over the past 100 years have limited their thinking to the analytic and utilitarian, reducing strategic ideas to initiatives about saving costs and efficiency while ignoring the creative and intuitive.

This balance between right and left brain thinking is hard to achieve – it is a messy, iterative process. Another theme shared with earlier chapters – diversity – pops up here as an essential for leaders' and managers' attention. Design thinkers also encourage *active* engagement with *the* strategic problem; with consumers, with users and with potential solutions. So the process is more than thinking – it is also about building diverse teams of people, actively observing the problem first-hand, role playing, constructing prototypes early, trying, failing and trying again.

Design thinkers, who are truly great at their art, do it because they seek elegant, entirely new strategic solutions that balance *commercial* with *meaningfully better*. They are craftsmen who build and create not *just* to make money. There is a balance of purpose as well as a balance of minds.

Designed by humans for humans

Chapters 5 and 6 take a deep dive into human nature and make the case for designing natural solutions to both strategic decision-making processes and organisational structures.

Chapter 5 – 'Behavioural Strategy' – describes how human beings really make decisions. It discounts the assumptions in economic theory that we are in control of our decisions and make them rationally most of the time. In fact how we behave is often irrational and strongly influenced by our emotions, our subconscious and the environment we are in. Therefore how we behave has a huge effect on organisational strategy, much of which has been ignored by strategists in the past.

Understanding our natural behaviour, as determined by how our brains work, is important not only in its own right but also because it explains why so many of the other topics in this book are vital to effective strategy-making. For example our preferred way to think and behave is optimistically, as if we are certain, confident and in control. The flip side is thinking about uncertainty and the unknown, which stimulate feelings of anxiety that we usually want to avoid. These preferences, *for* control and *against* uncertainty, mean that we are not naturally inclined to take the advice of the complexity theorists and the scenario planners and scan unknown worlds or uncertain parts of our businesses and landscapes; rather we stay on the ground that we assume is certain and assured – a dangerous place strategically.

So if we want to make better strategic decisions the prescription is twofold: to force ourselves into places that are often difficult, uncomfortable and challenging, and to design and engage with strategy processes that are much more robust in the face of our natural behaviour. One such process is design thinking. Others, also common themes throughout the book, are promotion of curiosity, contrary voices and diversity of mind, removing formality and hierarchy, releasing energy and stepping outside – often, and to places that are different and challenging and, placing one solid stake in the ground that is unequivocal about the identity and purpose of the organisation. With these, better decisions can be made.

Chapter 6 – 'Strategy and Human Nature' – continues with the theme of natural psychology but turns our attention to community and how people work most effectively and efficiently together and therefore gain competitive advantage. The characteristics of natural communities are quite different from the machine-like bureaucracies that have become commonplace within our organisations today, especially in the large ones that are often heralded as being the most successful.

Natural communities are structured as small clans because size dictates how people relate to each other and make meaning of themselves, their histories and the work they do collectively. Natural relationships are founded on reciprocity (not targets). Individuals make commitments among themselves to participate and contribute to the overall effort of the clan where they have the best match of capability (this is not decided for them by the organisation). Groups are diverse. Leaders emerge, chosen largely by followers (not bosses) who can sense those who are the most talented for specific roles and/or those who are the most trustworthy. People and roles are flexible and responsive to the needs of the whole clan and the environment, and individuals are responsible for themselves *as well as* the whole clan at the same time – they appreciate both the benefits and costs of collaboration and being able to see for themselves that the balance falls on the side of community living. Ownership, therefore, is an important concept; having the purpose of existing to make money for someone else, as shareholder value might be perceived, is not a motivating or inspiring psychological contract.

Because so much that is natural about how people want to be in relationships and work together is alien to the way many businesses and organisations choose to arrange themselves, this chapter provides extensive case studies about two 'human' companies. These are examples of businesses which are commercially successful *because* they put people first. The role of the stewards and leaders of these organisations is to maintain the ongoing health of their living companies, which are innovative, creative, growing systems. Here strategy emerges as a result of the *structure* of the organisation and not the other way round.

Revealing assumptions

In Chapters 7 and 8, Katie Best and Gill Ereaut reveal assumptions about strategy and about deep organisational beliefs, respectively.

In Chapter 7 – 'Strategy As Practice' – we discover the work of a new, young field of research which, unlike the other topics, does not start from a body of established theory. Instead, this academic approach is itself upended and the academics set out not to find evidence in support of their theories, but to observe the reality of practice.

From these observations, we see that if the 'taken-for-granteds' are challenged, quite a different view can emerge. For example the inanimate document that is labelled the strategy or the plan, somehow along the way, has assumed primacy over the activity of strategising. Simply shifting the focus, changing the word from a noun to a verb – 'strategy' to 'strategise' – redirects attention to people and process, where there is huge richness and possibility.

Also, in common with the complexity perspective, this chapter illustrates how phrases like the one we met earlier – 'we are spending too much time **in** the business rather than **on** the business' – need a healthy challenge. The SAP perspective argues that the people in the business are all strategic actors and that strategy happens at all levels, all the time. So often strategy is seen only as big-picture, high-level thinking, but the SAP work alongside the complexity view reminds us how excellence is amplified from local, individual practice to the whole. It reminds us that the whole is only a constituent of its parts. And that *just one bad apple* means that strategy is also about the detail, about the mundane and about execution in equal measure with formulation.

Gill Ereaut describes in Chapter 8 – 'Strategy and Discourse' – the power of language in creating the reality we inhabit within organisations. She uses her methodology of rigorously analysing the internal discourse to reveal the deep assumptions that determine the cultural aspects of an organisation: who we are, what matters around here, which groups of people are important and what we believe in.

Culture matters because it is a stabilising influence on an organisation, restricting agility and flexibility. The habits and routines of people working together are shared and, as they are copied, become ingrained, taken for granted and, eventually, invisible to insiders. These behaviours co-evolve with an organisation's collective mindset, where they are held as beliefs and values, and are largely subconscious and hard to change. Culture can, therefore, influence strategic formulators and limit strategic implementation, especially if values and beliefs need to be adapted. Because of culture, organisations can fall significantly out of line with customer needs, become irrelevant in the market space and lose their competitive advantage.

Chapter 8 makes culture tangible, which is in itself helpful, but it also goes further. Language is an artefact of culture, one that is pervasive and illustrative of the repetitive and dominant behaviours of an organisation. As with deeply held assumptions, the habitual internal discourse can become 'silent' and unheard, and when it does, it is hard for incumbents to locate strategic blocks and leaves the organisation groping for the right levers to make change happen. Discourse analysis provides an answer. It can be used to uncover the reasons for cultural resistance. In Gill's experience, revealing silent assumptions is a 'light bulb' moment. Almost instantly people can identify with their own 'stuck' behaviour and have the energy to make change happen, because there is clarity about what to do about it.

Process matters

One of the lessons Katie draws from the strategy as practice field of study is that shifting emphasis to *strategising* – the process – will bring strategic benefits. Much of the design-thinking topic (Chapter 4) supports this, emphasising the importance of process to finding elegant and imaginative strategic solutions. This is resoundingly affirmed in Chapter 9, where Lewis Pinault brings his extensive and intimate experience as a complexity thinker and 'play specialist' to the topic – 'Strategy as Serious Play'.

Chapter 9 shows how many of the themes and recommendations discussed so far can be incorporated into a process that is very different from the typical 'talking shops' that strategy meetings have become. Serious play sessions change the medium from flat two-dimensional paperwork and Powerpoint slides to constructed models – a three-dimensional experience. Metaphor and story are used extensively (Chapters 3 and 4), emotional input and social interaction is encouraged (Chapter 6), individual input is respected and promoted above hierarchy which is reduced to the minimum (Chapters 5–7), complexity and ambiguity are built into the modelling and storytelling (Chapters 2–4), right-brain thinking and left-brain thinking are a natural outcome of the design of the physical hands-on activities (Chapters 4 and 5), formality is reduced – and the process is fun. People leave play workshops with a deep insight and understanding of complex strategic problems, ownership and commitment to the resolution and the direction *from here*. A serious play workshop can reveal assumptions (Chapters 7 and 8) and be used to help organisations reimagine their culture and identities and thus enable fundamental change.

In charge but not in control

Chapter 10 – 'Strategy as Social Process' – is the book's anchor. If you start here, or start and finish here, you will get a sense of many of the themes common throughout the book, albeit from an organisational and socially complex view.

Bill explains the past, summing up why today's dominant managerial discourse is akin to the engineering metaphor of the controllable, simple and rule-based. He strips away many of these traditional assumptions and explains why messiness, informality and degrees of instability are important to long-run, complex problems that are strategic. He makes clear the two main themes of strategy – formulating intentions and responding to the consequences of strategic action – and shows that the here and now, the local and the collective wisdom of the whole are *all* important. He argues that informal messiness should be legitimised and elevated to equal status with the formal and that to do this leaders must recognise the paradox that while they are responsible, they are not always or totally in control of what is a constantly evolving complex system of people interacting with each other.

Roaming over the new landscape

The topics in this book are taken from different fields of research. The language, words and terms used for each are different, but the ideas and prescriptions have much in common, all of which promote the messy and informal, the creative and innovative, the experimental and discovering, the ownership and democratisation of *strategising* to be equal in stature to the planned/engineering paradigm that has dominated thinking over the past 60 or more years. We know that the status quo is hard to shake off, but we also know that crises and periods of instability stimulate curiosity and provide energy and momentum to explore and break old habits. As we write (2012), we are living through a crisis and inertia is broken, this book provides a rich collection of ideas and choices about how to move on.

Over to you … Enjoy!

2
Strategy for a Complex World

Jean Boulton

Introduction

The world is increasingly interconnected, multi-faceted and unpredictable. Operations in the world are more-and-more wide-reaching. Many businesses have an almost global sweep, and many not-for-profit non-governmental organisations cover vast terrains. Economic patterns pervade the entire globe as does the impact of climate change, limitations in mineral resources, social inequality and unrest. And yet the dominant scientific and professional methodologies still act as if the future is predictable and stable, as if plans and strategies can be built on past success. And as if such plans, when implemented, lead to the expected outcomes. But is this really our experience? How often are strategies implemented as intended, and, if they are, how often do they achieve the intended goals? We live in a complex, fast-changing and dynamic world. How can organisations face this complexity successfully, both in the longer-term as well as the short-term? In this chapter we explore what the theory of complexity has to offer such strategic concerns, what guidance and insights it can provide.

What is complexity theory?

Complexity theory has its roots in the work of physicists and biologists and systems thinkers in the early 20th century, in particular in the work of Ilya Prigogine (Allen and Boulton 2011). Prigogine was intrigued as to why classical physics gives a view of the world as predictable and controllable whereas evolutionary theory shows that the natural world evolves into new species with new qualities. He realised that, if you looked at the physics of *open* rather than *closed* systems, physics and biology come into agreement. He showed how new patterns and structures can emerge without design. What emerges is shaped by history, but in ways that are not easily open to prediction.

In Summary

- Organisations and markets and economies are complex – emergent, evolutionary, systemic and contingent on the detailed history of actions, events and decisions
- Complexity theory provides a new scientific perspective on what it means to say that the world – and organisations – are complex
- It brings into question the efficacy of prediction and control
- It brings a change of emphasis when it comes to strategy and leadership – more participation, a recognition of the potential for both lock-in and tipping points, greater recognition of the inevitability of uncertainty and the need for diversity of approach

---

Complexity theory provides a scientific theory of such open systems. A *system* conveys the notion of a group of interacting elements, and an *open system* can exchange information and energy with its environment. Organisations – and indeed markets and economies – can be considered as examples of complex systems – a bunch of people relating and inter-relating – exchanging information, services and goods, affecting and being affected by the broader context and environment, by the wider world.

This organic, emergent, systemic, path-dependent view of the world is much more relevant to organisations and markets than is the traditional image of the organisation or market as *machine* – where strategies (we are told) can be researched, planned, executed and measured, and success will surely follow.

How and what do we know about the behaviour of complex systems? The main method used to gain insight into open complex systems has been mathematical modelling, and such modelling has provided various and varying perspectives as to how such systems behave. Whilst not every sort of model provides identical conclusions, there are certain key features on which there is general agreement. Complexity theorists would agree that complex systems:

- **Are organic**
  - Complex systems have more in common with ecosystems, with evolving organisms than with machines; they are not in general predictable or programmable.

- **Are comprised of self-organising patterns of relationships**
  - Complex systems often display patterns or structures which can be relatively stable but still display some variation and fluctuating behaviour and may indeed evolve, eventually, into some new patterns.

- **Have a path-dependent future**
  - The future depends on the *detail* of what happens, does not smoothly follow from the past. Knowledge of the future in the form of accurate predictions based on the present does not exist, no matter how much we know, how clever are our methods and how comprehensive our data. Rather multiple possible futures exist.

- **Are affected by multiple causes**
  - In general there are not simple cause-and-effect chains; outcomes are influenced by several factors acting together – affected by chance, impacted by many local interactions, constrained by current patterns of relationships, shaped by the past and sensitive to occurrences in the wider environment.

- **Have connections which are non-linear, leading to change being spasmodic**
  - Sometimes current patterns are locked-in and hard to budge, sometimes change can be fast and radical, sometimes patterns are flexible and adaptable and resilient.

- **Are emergent**
  - Sometimes change can lead to the emergence of features qualitatively different from those of the past.

Stability or 'tipping' into new regimes?

The complex world as seen through the lens of complexity theory is summarised in the following diagram which encapsulates the dilemma facing all managers. Is the present situation *stable*, and can we make sense of the identifiable patterns of relationships between identifiable factors? Or will events and new entrants, new innovations or shifts in the broader environment, change the rules of the game, *tip* us into something new?

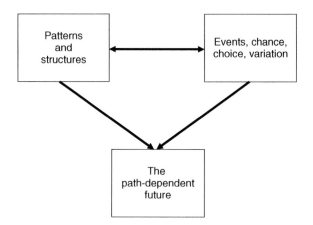

When situations are relatively stable, then the market or economy can be analysed in terms of current, measurable and relatively stable *patterns* of relationships. So economists can, in principle, measure supply and demand curves and set prices; marketers can undertake market research and gain understanding of what kind of people will buy what kind of products at what price; programme managers in the third sector can understand the patterns of livelihood and culture. New product or service strategies – where these are extensions of what currently exists – can be planned and implemented with relative effectiveness.

However, complexity theory shows us that *events* – new entrants, or shocks, or chance or changes in social norms – can destabilise current patterns and structures and lead to a future which is radically different; where, after a period of relative chaos, new alliances and buying patterns can become established which can be radically different from those in the past. These *events* may be prosaic, such as a celebrity choking on your product or, more positively, wearing a dress you designed or championing the cause of your charity. Events may be the result of shifts in relationships between institutions due to leaders moving on or people changing allegiance. They may be caused by changes in the law or catalysed by innovation or result from global environmental disasters, war or famine. Changes in patterns and relationships may also shift through more gradual drifts in public opinion that go on under the surface with little to show and then suddenly erupt in changed attitudes and behaviour. The shift into recycling in the UK a few years ago had this quality; moved from being accepted only by the few to being adopted by the majority in a few short years.

Complexity theory sees the future as derived from the interplay *between* the detailed history of *events* and the currently established *patterns and structures*, potentially destabilising such patterns. So, in times of stability, understanding current patterns and structures will give a good indication of likely outcomes and will allow planning and foresight. In times of gross instability critical events will predominantly shape what happens. In general outcomes are a complex combination of the interplay between the two. As Prigogine (Prigogine, Allen et al. 1977: 39) said:

> Thus we find a natural expression of the idea that societies function as a machine – referring to the deterministic periods between instabilities, and society as being dominated by 'critical events' (e.g. 'great men') which occur at the points of instability.

The point is that the future *is not* in general incrementally built on the past; the future may be *radically* different from what has been the norm previously. Whilst we cannot know for sure whether we are in a period of stability or near a so-called tipping point, it can be necessary to exercise judgement in order to maximise our chances of success. To what extent can we assume the present is relatively stable and will be a good map through which to navigate the future, where success may indeed be driven by understanding the way things currently work and being intelligent about how to work within current patterns? Or are we in a period of instability, where success is driven by readiness for a new future and by attempting to envisage and shape and adapt to what emerges? Informing such judgements is a key part of strategy development.

What does this mean for strategy development

If, as we suggest, a market or economy displays these features of a complex system, then managers are presented with a new scientific justification as to why strategies, however well-researched and conceived and implemented, may not achieve what was planned. Although the future is not random, the future *is* affected by many interacting factors. What happens next depends in part on the *detail* of what happens and on how behaviours – both internal and external – work together. As we have indicated, the future may not just be a little different from what was expected, it may be quite different. Think of the effect of text messaging on the mobile phone industry. It was not a planned strategy (it was developed as a way of testing phones remotely) and companies never anticipated it would grow so rapidly and contribute to the emergence of a new teenage market for mobile phones, and become a key tool for business communication.

And how long will success last for even the greatest organisations? There have been a number of books that identify exemplary companies, for example, *In Search of Excellence* (Peters and Waterman 1982) and *Good to Great* (Collins 2001). How many of these organisations would still be regarded as exemplary? Some no longer even exist. Can we really ever reliably identify salient factors that will lead to success both now and in the future? Can we 'roll-out' planned strategies and follow recipes and formulae (even good ones), or do we need a change of mindset?

Complexity thinking provides such a new mindset and provides some insights into the process of strategy development, as we discuss in the sections below.

Take a portfolio approach

Complexity thinking emphasises the need for a portfolio approach. This is driven by the recognition that the market displays differing levels of stability and consequent uncertainty, as sketched out in the diagram below.

Increasing instability

Starting at the left-hand side of the diagram, some elements of your business are likely to be stable and the name of the game is *efficiency*. Life insurance is a good example of a quite stable predictable business stream; it is relatively easy to predict death rates and relatively easy to predict the sort of questions claimants will ask.

Other elements of your business may be new to *you* but not really pioneering in the market, and as such are unlikely to change market dynamics. You are extrapolating, *extending* from what you know. You may try to sell green kettles where you have previously sold red kettles, or provide services to a new geographical region abutting a region where you already operate. So there may be more uncertainty than in the region of efficiency, but this uncertainty is something that can be researched and contained.

Thirdly, you may be dealing with issues of *fashion*, where the underlying dynamics of the market may fluctuate but the average qualities of the market do not change. That is to say, taking shoes as an example, whilst the size of the shoe market is relatively stable, which *fashion* of shoe will sell in any given year is harder to predict. Malcolm Gladwell (2000) in his book *Tipping Point* tells the story of Hush Puppy shoes. These shoes had been popular in the 1970s and 1980s, but by 1994 sales were down to 30,000 pairs. Then suddenly, for no apparent reason, they started to be regarded as 'hip' in the clubs and bars of downtown Soho in New York. The few remaining outlets that still sold the shoes were starting to sell out. Then a couple of designers used them on the catwalk. The directors of the company who owned Hush Puppy were totally taken aback by this sudden demand but they did react, and by 1995 the company was selling 430,000 pairs a year. The story both shows how public opinion and word of mouth can cause a product to take off – in this case for a second time – but also shows that such trends can be fickle. This growth did not last and taste moved on to pastures new.

Finally, there is the region of 'unknown unknowns' where markets may shift radically and rapidly and new features may *emerge*. This region differs from the fashion market where markets fluctuate but do not necessarily result in radical change.

In this region of 'unknown unknowns' some products have the potential to destabilise and catalyse reformation of the market. Examples are often, but not always, fuelled by new technology such as the Internet or optical fibre technology. Some strategists and business leaders sense the potential to create a new market or react quickly when the 'pull' of the consumer shows a new market is emerging. Some strategists are adept at building on shifting social trends such as interest in health issues, captured by Innocent with their Smoothie, or, even more interestingly, by the explosion in the selling of bottled water which links to healthy lifestyles and to fears of pollution by impurities. Indeed one could argue that bottled water is a triumph of marketing over matter. Volumes have risen 12% a year since the 1970s and sells, in about 60 % of cases, filtered tap water. It is hardly a product at all and certainly not innovative technologically. It is in this regime of unknown unknowns where it is hard to predict what will happen and risks are effectively impossible to characterise or quantify.

Of course this move into 'unknown unknowns' may not necessarily be catalysed by *your* product; it may be the result of someone else's innovation, or it may have nothing to do with products or innovations at all but may be the result of turbulence or sudden shifts in the wider environment due to political change or economic recession or environmental disasters.

So business strategies which rely on a hope that the present will last forever will inevitably fail in the end, no matter how efficiently products and services are delivered. And the timing of the demise of the cash cow or the duration of success in products and services at the whim of fashion or the duration of currently stable patterns and norms in the social and natural environment is always hard, if not impossible, to predict. It is thus important to have a portfolio approach – to extend markets and products in new directions and to take some risks, test out the market with fresh ideas, fresh supply chains, fresh approaches.

Experiment, seize opportunities and adapt to changing circumstances

Complexity thinking positions strategy development as more provisional and encourages experimentation. If we truly believe that strategies must be more provisional, contingent on the dynamic nature of the market, we are likely to review progress more often, to regard failure as part of learning, to act more quickly to seize opportunities and to modify intentions and implementations. We accept we have to 'learn by doing', that we cannot always know what will be successful.

Examples of companies that failed by overly believing their own research and 'betting the farm' are explored in a very interesting way by Christensen (1997) in *The Innovator's Dilemma*. For example, Christensen describes how Hewlett Packard, in 1991, developed a small 1.3-inch disk drive. The company had very ambitious growth plans and felt there was a new market looming for the technology – hand-held palm-top computers. Market research confirmed this and HP went ahead and developed a sophisticated product which seemed to meet the expected market requirement. In the event, sales were small and in fact were in a completely different market – Japanese-language portable word processors, miniature cash registers and electronic cameras – none of which had figured in their marketing plans. Then they started receiving enquiries from firms making mass-market video games, but needing a lower price point than the current product. Unfortunately HP could not easily lower the functionality of the disk drive and thus lower the price. In retrospect they felt they should have been more wary of market forecasts for emerging markets and not got locked-in to large-scale and inflexible manufacturing capacity. They felt they should have taken a much more flexible and exploratory approach.

There are also success stories. Some of these are fuelled no doubt by entrepreneurial skill; some are fuelled by luck and some result from seizing opportunities when they present themselves. And indeed some are the result of unintended consequences of actions taken for other reasons. For example, as already discussed, text messaging was not a planned strategy, but took off as a result of engineers in Nokia developing a technique for testing mobile phones remotely. One Christmas one of the engineers sent a Merry Christmas text to his colleagues and suddenly everyone was interested. The technology grew as a result of the enormous 'pull' from the public, particularly young teenagers; initially it was not 'pushed' at all.

Another example is found in the consequences of the huge growth and popularity of social networking sites. Recruitment agencies have adapted and seized the opportunity to use sites such as LinkedIn to advertise and search for new recruits – thus saving themselves money but also increasing effectiveness as they align themselves with the popular social processes of communication.

There are many stories of the demise of organisations that do not change with the times and do not respond to shifting expectations, new entrants and new technologies. For example, *The Economist* (2012) ran an article in January 2012 comparing the demise of Kodak with the continuing success of Fujifilm. Their analysis pointed to the difficulty of shifting mindsets and cultures within Kodak as being a key factor in limiting their ability to respond to shifting trends. They quote Rosabeth Moss Kanter (a Harvard Business School Professor, who worked with the company) as saying. Kodak 'suffered from a mentality of perfect products rather than [an attitude of] "make it, launch it, fix it" '. Fujifilm, they say, was fleeter of foot, seized opportunities, was more adept at reading the changing trends in the market, and recognising the power of the new entrants, the computer companies starting to manufacture digital cameras.

Use foresighting and scenario planning

As Kodak found, the market is hard to call, not always as stable as we would like, subject to sudden shifts and the emergence of new features. But we should not regard market behaviour as random. There tend to be warning signs of increasing instability and signs of the likelihood of major change. So there is an important role in strategy development for *foresighting* (Clayton, Wehrmeyer et al. 2003), for scanning the horizon for signs of impending change and for evidence of new innovations or shocks or new entrants that have the potential to reshape the market. *Scenario planning* (Schwartz 1999) is an important tool that helps us to imagine a number of possible futures, building on information but also on instinct and imagination. Scenario planning does not require us to decide on one particular future; it allows us to play with futures which may be not very likely but which would create a radically different future if they did occur (Craven 2009). We can then look for evidence of shifts towards our different scenarios and act accordingly as we see what starts to emerge.

We also may be able to modify our current approaches to give the potential for adapting did one of these more radical but unlikely scenarios occur. For example, what will the long-term effect of digital media be on the music industry? How will the publishing industry survive the impact of e-books and private publishing? Did we or could we have anticipated the rise of the Arab Spring? Are we factoring the implications of climate change into our thinking? Or do we, to quote John Gray (2009), tend to believe in a 'breathless continuation of the present'. That is to say, do we implicitly assume, in our approach to strategy development, that the characteristics of today's world will last for the foreseeable future?

Manage by walking about

Implementers of strategy are often the people who are first in touch with what is and is not working, who sense any changing patterns of behaviour before they can be proven, who are in tune with the nuances of geographical and demographical differences in patterns of purchasing and consuming. The reality of the contingent and emergent nature of behaviour re-affirms the importance of 'managing by walking about', a phrase originally coined by executives in Hewlett Packard. There may be unexpected successes emerging that were not intended but can usefully be nurtured; there may be a need to connect up people and resources and facilitate synergies. There may also be a need to change or modify direction if the current intentions are just not working out. So strategy development and strategy implementation become much more closely entwined.

Weave clear intentions globally, plan locally

In an uncertain world, which is complex and contingent on local factors, it is increasingly impossible to act as if strategic plans can be far-reaching into the future, or can be applied universally and uniformly over the whole market. The *local context* has many specific features and factors particular to local circumstances. This is not to say that strategies need be weak or tentative. Decisive action is often an advantage in shaping new markets, seizing the advantage. So how do we act coherently and decisively and yet respond to local contexts? The advice is to clarify strategic intentions, indeed develop them, 'weave' them together with many stakeholders with different perspectives to ensure they are both well-informed and 'owned' by those that matter. Nevertheless, although contained by these strategic intentions, allow detailed planning to take place more locally. Such local strategies and approaches can be standardised to some extent by setting up processes for sharing learning and reviewing so that intelligence and experience reflexively improves what is done and leads to a degree of coherence. The importance of responding to the local context has long been promoted, on the one hand, by proponents in International Development, for example Chalmers (1997), and, on the other, by organisations such as HSBC 'the world's local bank'.

As well as local variation, it is highly likely that the contexts and salient aspects of the markets and the wider economy and social trends will themselves *change over time*. So reliance on detailed long-term plans can create more harm than good in that such an approach does not create a mindset of adaptation and can blinker us to noticing evidence of unexpected success as well as to failure. Adopting regular review processes, *expecting* things not to go to plan can be fruitful attitudes to the strategy process.

Think systemically

We are so used to approaching organisation and markets as if they are mechanical, as if they can be reduced into separate parts and as if outcomes are clearly and causally related to specific inputs that it is easy to forget that situations are really forged by many factors working synergistically. So, strategies work best if they can take into account and respond to a wide perspective. Sales of one product will be affected by sales of quite different products as people choose on what to spend their discretionary income. Recession or social unrest or loss of confidence can destabilise buying habits or fracture livelihoods quickly and sharply. Equally, it is easy to miss opportunities for collaboration or synergy if thinking is too linear or blinkered. Could delivery vans deliver products for more than one supplier at the same time? Could public libraries be used more extensively for other public services?

The NGOs in the International Development sector give examples where systemic thinking has been constrained by the at times narrow focus of funders; where you have new schools but no teachers or new crops but no transport.

And there are also some great examples of success too. For example, M-PESA is a mobile-phone-based money transfer system, launched in 2007. It is now the most used money transfer service in Kenya. Why has it been so successful? Johnson (2011) explains that it is because it harmonises and works with existing networks of interpersonal lending and enables long-standing cultural processes of reciprocal support. With many people now working away from the village, money can easily be sent home. The success then is because the technology is congruent with existing systemic processes. It supports rather than re-engineers.

If global organisations can allow greater local autonomy, then those nearest to the action can build up alliances, work in tune with local conditions and respond adaptively. In the search for efficiency business organisations and NGOs want to standardise, they want to achieve economies of scale. This can work against knitting together local strands and responding to local concerns, needs, opportunities and threats. It can lead to a hollow *efficiency* of use of resources without a consequent *effectiveness* of strategic implementation.

Beware the beguiling goal of dominance

One very interesting topic to consider is the issue of dominance. Dominant organisations are able to simplify their markets, make suppliers and supply chains and even consumers act in the way that suits them. Indeed an unregulated market, as discussed by complexity economist Brian Arthur (1994), tends to allow the big to get bigger and the dominant to get more dominant. Such mega-organisations are able to assert a simplified and unassailable machine-like process on the world which is to their advantage. Smaller organisations disappear, diversity of approach and choice is reduced. This power of dominance is very beguiling for business, and many business organisations might wish to achieve this position, build barriers to entry, lock-out any competition. But whilst such dominance can 'win' in the short term or even the medium term, such organisations are less able to adapt to changing circumstances. They may be more efficient but they are less resilient. If consumer choice shifts, if there are new innovations, or if new entrants judge the preferences of the market more accurately, then such locked-in organisations are likely to fail and to fail catastrophically.

Equally, dominant mega-organisations might not be in the public's best interests as they tend to lead to reduction in choice and competition. And, through being too large to govern, the profit motive is unfettered and may squeeze out due attention to social and environmental concerns. The triumph of petrol cars over electric cars is one such example. It is said that if Henry Ford had liked electric cars then the automobile industry and its impact on the oil industry and on climate change could have been very different (Geels 2005). Now, given the extensive infrastructure that supports petrol cars, the locked-in interests of shareholders and executives, the oil industry continues to extract oil in ever more dangerous and environmentally questionable terrains. The move towards more carbon-efficient transport is hard to achieve.

Issues of power and dominance also play out in politics and of course in the interplay between politics and business. A recent article in *New*

Scientist (2012) tells of massive engineering works planned on the Niger River sanctioned by the Malian government. This will provide water for the South African sugar giant Illovo and a Chinese State enterprise but is likely to create drought which will lead to failed fishing, dying cattle and hence force more than a million people into migration. Equally, international organisations such as the World Bank have enormous power to uphold the ideology of free markets and insist on the abolishment of trade barriers and subsidies in exchange for loans (Wade 2011). Meanwhile, subsidies to cotton framers in the US severely disadvantage cotton producers in Mali and Burkino Faso (Fairtrade Foundation 2010).

One key factor in creating dominance is advertising. Clearly advertising has great power to change social norms in that it works not only with reason but also trades on emotions, and is opportunistic in seizing opportunities afforded by current and local events, by actions of celebrities and emerging trends. Indeed advertising specialists, lobbyists and campaign organisers are in many ways natural complexity thinkers.

But there is an issue of *values* that this raises. For example, the escalating consumer drive for novelty, the desire for more of everything, can be laid at the feet of the marketing strategist. On the one hand this has a positive impact on growth, on the other it sits with increasing difficulty in a world where carbon emissions and populations are still growing whilst resources – of land and water as well as oil and minerals – are diminishing. So the emphasis on the systemic and emergent nature of the future pins an ethical responsibility on the strategist. You are not merely increasing the profits of your company but you have the potential to change the world irreversibly and not necessarily for the better.

This also raises the issue of regulation and governance. If, as Arthur (1994) suggests, there is a natural tendency in a free market for the rich to get richer and the powerful to get more powerful, for diversity and choice to diminish, then is there not a need for regulation to counter this tendency, uphold the voice of the powerless and place value on the longer term? This is an unpopular topic but one requiring fresh consideration (Boulton 2010).

The NGO sector faces particular issues in respect of dominance. They are expected by donors and the general public to prove the efficacy of use of funds with clear and unassailable measurements of well-identified outcomes achieved in ever-shorter timescales. There is a machine-like expectation for certainty and evidence. But of course the places in the world most in need of help tend to be particularly complex, prone to fast-change and hard to understand. The drive for 'evidence' can lead to pressure to impose and standardise solutions, to simplify problems, to work on single issues – in a sense to mimic the methods of business. Yet NGOs are not seeking to dominate but to support, work with, empower. NGOs have to somehow manage the tension between the machine-like expectations for evidence and to respond to the needs of the least powerful and most disadvantaged in the locally specific, synergistic, chaotic and complex contexts in which they operate.

So complexity theory emphasises the limitations and dangers of dominance. For businesses, too great a focus on short-term profits may weaken your own competitive advantage in the future, and this is not to mention the impact it can have on the wider concerns of choice and social trends. And NGOs and their funders need to continue the conversation as to how to demonstrate impact and effectiveness whilst grappling with realities of very complex contexts.

Find synergies between inner and outer

There are many theories of strategy development. Mintzberg's (1998) book, *The Strategy Safari*, gives a very comprehensive review of the different approaches. Some theories advocate building on strengths, some focus on learning and adaptation, some of course adhere to the detailed planning approach we have been keen, here, to bring into question. What we have emphasised in this chapter is the importance of experimenting, of judging the level of instability in the market and broader environment, of binding people together through weaving strong intentions and yet adapting to signs of change. The complexity message is about *balance*: between finding what works and catalysing innovation and change, between intention and responsiveness, between foresight and pragmatism. The complexity approach would emphasise the need to explore, reflexively, the synergies between the *inner* – the strengths and expertise, reputation and resources and interests and capabilities of an organisation – and the *outer* – the market, the competition, the future, the issues of the wider environment. The organisation must be market-led but weave this market intelligence and judgement of the future together with an assessment of its capabilities and competitive advantages. Too great a focus on the market at the expense of an understanding of the capabilities of the organisation will not work of itself. Such synergistic couplings in a dynamic market rely on judgement as well as analysis and do depend heavily on experience, instincts and foresight.

Conclusion

If managers and politicians and policy makers truly believed that the world was complex, inter-dependent, with a future that is largely impossible to predict, they would need little persuasion to modify practices and processes and make different judgement calls. We need to shift what is accepted as the underlying science that drives what is deemed professional. Acting as if the world is measurable, controllable and predictable when it is not does not make it so. And yet neither is the world chaotic and random; there are patterns of relationships; there are market dynamics and patterns in demography and economic and political behaviour. The issue of judgement is about how stable and universal are such patterns, how we anticipate impending change and how we respond to emerging futures that may have many different features compared with the past. Complexity thinking does not throw away every management practice, but it *does* change our attitude as to how to use them, to their likely success and to the relative emphasis on focusing on stability rather than handling uncertainty, novelty and change.

As Allen et al. (2011: 3) say: 'both the dream of omnipotence and the nightmare of impotence in a fully knowable but deterministic world dissolve with complexity science'.

Complexity thinking, in emphasising the inter-connectedness of the social, economic and political world, also warns against too blinkered a focus on the short term and on profit and success. If organisations destroy the world on which they depend, if organisations squeeze suppliers to too great a degree, use up finite resources or if governments make political choices that are insensitive to the long term, our short-term, profit-driven and efficient machine will destroy its markets and its environment.

Complexity thinking also raises the question as to the need for regulation and governance – to limit the size and reach of global organisations and to uphold the voice of the disadvantaged and the longer-term environmental considerations. Complexity thinking shows the need for greater diversity in organisation purpose, and brings attention to the effect of too great a focus on short-term shareholder value at the expense of long-term consideration of the market and the wider social and environmental world. How can the drive of global business be tempered with the needs of the disadvantaged, of the future, of the changing environment? Even through the lens of a strictly business focus, comprising the future will not lead to continuing business success. Complexity thinking, with its message of emergence, is often used to justify de-regulation, but we would disagree with this. As history shows, that which emerges unhindered is not necessarily in the best interests of the future.

So, in summary:

- Take a portfolio approach; the future is not easily predictable and dominant cash cows can be prone to sudden death.
- Experiment and then build on what works.
- See intelligence-gathering as a continuous and systemic process, both inside the organisation and in the wider world.
- See strategy as live, responsive and adaptive.
- Take care of the longer term; resist too great a focus on short-term profits at the expense of the future.
- Make *judgements,* based on foresighting, 'walking about' as well as analysis; the future in general does not follow smoothly from the present.
- Allow local response rather than insist on standardisation, but inform this by shared principles and intentions.

References

Allen, P. and Boulton, J. (2011). Complexity and Limits to Knowledge: The Importance of Uncertainty, in P. Allen, S. Maguire and B. McKelvey, *Sage Handbook of Complexity and Management*, London: Sage.

Allen, P. et al. (2011). Editorial, in P. Allen, S. Maguire and B. McKelvey, *Sage Handbook of Complexity and Management*, London: Sage.

Arthur, W.B. (1994). *Increasing Returns and Path Dependence in the Economy*, Michigan: University of Michigan Press.

Boulton, J. (2010). Complexity Theory and Implications for Policy Development. *Emergence: Complexity and Organisation* 12(2): 31–41.

Chalmers, R. (1997). *Whose Reality Counts? Putting the Last First*, London: Intermediate Technology Publications.

Christensen, C. (1997). *The Innovator's Dilemma*, Boston: Harvard Business School Press.

Clayton, A., Wehrmeyer, W. et al. (2003). *Foresighting for Development*, London: Earthscan Publications.

Collins, J.C. (2001). *Good to Great*, London: Random House.

Craven, G. (2009). *What's the Worst That Could Happen?* London: Penguin.

Economist (2012). *The Last Kodak Moment.* January 14th. Available at: http://www.economist.com/node/21542796 [Accessed February 12, 2012].

Fairtrade Foundation (2010). *The Great Cotton Stitch-up.* Available at: http://www.fairtrade.org.uk/includes/documents/cm_docs/2010/f/2_ft_cotton_policy_report_2010_loresv2.pdf [Accessed February 04, 2012].

Geels, F. (2005). The Dynamics of Transitions in Socio-technical Systems: A Multi-level Analysis of the Transition Pathway from Horse-drawn Carriages to Automobiles (1860–1930). *Technology Analysis & Strategic Management* 17(4): 445–476.

Gladwell, M. (2000). *The Tipping Point*, New York: Little Brown.

Gray, J. (2009). *False Dawn: The Delusions of Global Capitalism*, London: Granta Books.

Johnson, S. (2011). Understanding Kenya's Financial Landscape: The Missing Social Dimension. *FSD Kenya* 17.

Mintzberg, H. (1998). *Strategy Safari*, London: Financial Times Prentice Hall.

New Scientist (2012). *Aral Sea Disaster Will Be Repeated in Mali.* 24th March.

Peters, T. and Waterman, R. (1982). *In Search of Excellence*, New York: Harper and Row.

Prigogine, I., Allen, P. et al. (1977). *Long Term Trends and the Evolution of Complexity*, in E. Laszlo and J. Bierman, *Goals and a Global Community*, Vol. 1, New York: Pergamon Press.

Schwartz, P. (1999). *The Art of the Long View*, Chichester: Wiley.

Wade, R. (2011). *The Return of Industrial Policy. Economic Policies of the New Thinking in Economics.* T. C. T. f. N. T. i. Economics. Cambridge: St Catherine's College.

3
Strategy and the New Uncertainty

Robert Davies

The tyranny of the present

In 1983, Shell (the Dutch, global Oil and Gas Group) published their latest set of global scenarios. They were called Incrementalism and the Greening of Russia. The Greening of Russia told a tale about a virtually unknown man coming to power followed by a massive economic and political restructuring in Russia. It was not that this man, as an individual, would bring a halt to the Cold War. Rather that his arrival in power would be a symptom of a set of deep, underlying forces. When the scenario was shared with soviet experts in government agencies, they told Shell that this was as implausible as a fairy story.

The problem that the soviet experts had with Shell's story was one that is common to all of us. We live in the present and we form views of the world from our current reality. We make sense of the world by looking at it through eyes which reflect our own mental maps – our own paradigms. The world looks different according to the knowledge and experience we have, according to the thoughts that influence us and the way other people around us think. It is on the basis of this reality that managers make decisions and take actions.

Researchers call these mental maps 'interpretive schemes' which represent the values and interests of staff, particularly those of the top-level leadership teams in organisations, the key decision-makers. Critically, these interpretive schemes strongly influence the way in which both the external world and the organisation itself are seen and analysed (Ranson et al. 1980). Such 'mental maps' or 'interpretive schemes' act like massive filters or lenses that can distort or cut off views of what really is happening inside and outside the organisation. What this means in practice is that information about the outside world is heavily filtered, narrowed and even unknowingly re-manufactured by members of the organisation (Weick 1995). Interpretive schemes are at their most dangerous in mature organisations, where they are reinforced by myths and stories of 'what worked before'.

In stable environments, for short-term investments and in local situations, decisions based on current mindsets are likely to be as good as they can get. But, few companies would describe their current landscape as predictable and 'regular'. Indeed, the complex system that globalisation has produced is bound by its nature to produce 'catastrophic collapse' (Ferguson 2010). Therefore, we live in a time when turbulence and uncertainty are now common descriptors of our world.

This could well be the 'new normal'.

When complexity is fuelled by fast and wide connectivity, when investment decisions made today reap reward at some point in the future, there is a real chance that the foundation of decisions made using restrictive mental maps are, to say the least, shaky. They are 'shaky' because they are founded upon the interpretive schemes of the past and all too frequently, these decisions, unsurprisingly, prove to be defective. That is why strategists who need foresight turn to scenarios: to open minds, to attempt to break established 'interpretive schemes'. Scenarios are credible alternative worldviews which help challenge the deceit of certainty, enable managers to make better decisions and set a foundation for organisational exploration and learning.

Scenarios in practice

The fundamental starting point of scenario methodology is that the future is unknowable. Scenarios are plausible, challenging scripts – usually between two and four – that explore an unknowable future. They are not forecasts. They do not extrapolate from the past to predict what definitely will happen in the future, but instead they offer a range of very different stories of how the future could be. Scenarios, within a set, are all distinctly different; none of them are preferred or supply a strategy for the future. They make the thinker focus on uncertainty and do not aim for any resolution of this uncertainty. In these ways, scenarios are the antithesis of traditional approaches to business planning.

Shell is known for being the long-term practitioner and leading exponent of the technique. Pierre Wack was the original protagonist who devised the famous early 1970s scenarios (Wack 1985). At the time, he was one of Shell's central planning team and was persistently disappointed with the accuracy of the Group's future oil price forecasts. He became fascinated by the scenario methodology as an alternative to forecasting and adopted and developed it as a technique. Shell's approach diverged from those adopted by others which focused on quantitative data and computation of probabilities. This 'intuitive' methodology falls between model building and pure imagination, bringing quantitative data and qualitative ideas together in a mix of art and science (Verity 2003).

Shell's early scenarios dared to suggest that a dramatic rise in oil price might occur and when the 1973 barrel price rose from $1.70 to $40, the leaders of the Group believed they gained a decade of competitive advantage over rivals as a result of being mentally prepared and, as a result were, much faster to react. In the nineties, the Group scenario team identified three driving forces: globalisation, liberalisation and the influence of IT (the Internet specifically) which could not be excluded from either of their 1994 global scenarios (Shell nearly always produced only two stories about the future). This was the first time since Shell started building scenarios that a common root had to be acknowledged. This had a profound effect on leaders who felt a new sense of urgency about changing the strategic direction of the Group.

The process of building scenarios can bring many benefits to those who participate, including:

- preparing for discontinuities and unexpected change. These include Ferguson's 'catastrophic collapses';
- helping people to build a common language through which the future and its issues can be imagined, debated and shared;
- surfacing and changing individual, group and organisational mindsets (the interpretive schemes or mental maps introduced earlier);
- helping to integrate strong differences of opinion into stories that could result in unified action;
- helping to stimulate creative thinking and problem-solving;
- increasing agility and creating competitive advantage.

Over the past 40 years, governments, countries, think tanks and some very large organisations have invested in creating scenarios. But, until

2007–08, evidence of consistent, frequent use within organisations was limited. Often perceived as resource-intensive exercises that result in ambiguous outcomes, the deceptively stable business and political climate of the late 20th century and the early years of the 21st century did not appear to require tools that trawled widely, often to the edges of what seemed relevant to business, that looked for what might be unknown and that incorporated storytelling and imagination. Recently, however, following the Great Recession, there has been a resurgence of interest and a flurry of scenario-building activity.

However, the world has changed fundamentally as a result of globalisation, and this chapter questions if the scenario methodologies of the last century remain valid, and if not, what might prove a more relevant process. We conclude that whilst scenarios still do have a material role to play in helping business decision-makers grapple with uncertainty, an addition to the armoury is required. First, however, we will review the established scenario-building process and then introduce a new approach which will help organisations survive in a world of 'catastrophic collapses'.

Building scenarios

Time and expense are just two reasons for the low level of scenario use in organisations, another is that the process of building them is hard to explain. Several publications, including Ralston and Wilson (2006), Schwartz (2009) and Wilkinson (2009), have recently addressed this issue and describe a series of frequently used steps that have become generally available and accepted. These are as follows.

The place to start building scenarios is clarity about the overall focus, theme or issue that the organisation needs to address and a time-frame that is valid. Usually, a question is posed. By definition, this question cannot be answered using existing knowledge. In the case of a business, the question will usually identify the segment of the marketplace that will be explored. So, for example, Shell asks what the energy world will be like in 50 years time. At Cass our MBA students have built scenarios to answer questions like 'What role will London have as a global business centre in the year 2020?' and 'The Future of Work 2021: Implications for business leaders'.

Defining the question allows the main areas of research to be identified and information gathered. Research involves reading widely and talking with a broad range of interest groups, getting out and about and observing what is happening. The ability to listen and observe with an open mind, freed of the restrictions imposed by 'mental maps', is a key skill, as well as the imagination to talk with many people who have both diverse and challenging views. Usually the initial focus is upon understanding past events, trends and their underlying driving forces. A framework such as Political, Economic, Socio-demographic, Technological, Environmental and Legislative (PESTEL) is often applied to identify and categorise the 'driving forces' that produce change in the domain relevant to the scenario question.

At this point, it is important to note that the focus of this traditional process is upon 'driving forces' as opposed to identifying the human actors who must interpret and act upon such 'forces', an issue that we will return to later.

Past events and trends are analysed so that members of the scenario planning team can understand the role that driving forces have had in creating the world as we know it today.

The focus then moves to the future.

Using the PESTEL framework for classification purposes, the team proceeds to identify events and trends that it is certain will occur and excludes those that are irrelevant to answering the scenario question. The remaining critical certainties must, by definition, be included in any scenario that the team develops. The process is then repeated, but this time the team focuses upon identifying trends and events that it is uncertain about. The team, by definition, will know very little about these uncertainties but there will be agreement that if they did occur, the uncertainties would materially influence any answer to the scenario question. In a typical scenario-building workshop, it is not unusual to identify in excess of 50 uncertainties that are relevant to the scenario question. To manage this level of complexity, two processes of reduction are used next. The first of these involves team members grouping uncertainties that are felt to embrace similar features or characteristics together. A descriptor is then agreed to represent each group of uncertainties. These group descriptors are usually called 'super uncertainties'. This first process of reduction will typically produce between 6 and 10 groups of 'super uncertainties'.

The second process of reduction involves selecting two of the super uncertainties to provide the axes which separate different story-lines. Typically, each 'super uncertainty' relates to one of the PESTEL framework's forces. Therefore, the future is conceptualised with reference to only two elements, such as technology and environmentalism, or economic and legislative forces. In practice, therefore, emphasis is put on a subset of driving forces, a microcosm of the whole. The danger is that the final scenarios are dominated by consideration of a relatively small set of forces. This leaves the technique open to questions about over-simplification and reductionism. Can two axes really represent the complexity of the world that now confronts us?

The scenario stories are then built by aligning relevant variables against the extreme points of each axis, which produces a set of four scenario themes. Each theme is then developed, constructing plausible scripts from present day to the predetermined future time or scenario end point. Here critical skills are ones of synthesis and intuition, mixing the ability to pick important forces with likely variables and creating a logical story.

Scenarios are given distinctive and descriptive names that reflect each scenario's theme and characteristics.

A vital next step is to communicate them widely among decision-makers in the organisation. Without this, much of the value in the exercise is left untapped. Involvement from an early stage is the best way to communicate and get maximum value from the learning. If this is not possible, communication needs to make an impact on the mental schema of decision-makers, otherwise nothing will change.

Signals or 'early warning indicators' are then commonly identified for each scenario. These are events, factors or developments that could be monitored for after the scenarios are published and signal important aspects of the scenarios and possible further future possibilities.

Coping with catastrophic collapses?

Whilst many find the above process demanding, it can be used successfully to explore uncertainties and produce multiple views of the future, and these are capable of, in varying degrees, challenging the grip of established mental maps, or the 'tyranny of the past'.

There are however potential shortcomings, especially in the light of our now complex and interconnected world.

The first is the assumption that two 'super uncertainties' are sufficient to represent the global uncertainty that is possible today. Also, as we have observed, each of these 'super uncertainties' is itself only a microcosm of an underlying 'driving force'. Whilst this approach of using only a subset of two 'driving forces' may have had relevance in the pre-Internet, pre-globalisation age, today its rigour can be questioned. The scenarios that are produced by considering just two 'super uncertainties' might be artificially simplified abstractions of a far more complex environment. One way to overcome this is to produce more scenario sets, based on different combinations of all the 'super uncertainties', but in practice this produces an unmanageable range of scenarios for decision-makers to examine, aggregate and digest. And any organisation doing this would still be faced with the problem that each set of scenarios would tend towards a simplified abstraction.

The second reservation focuses upon the concept of building scenarios around 'driving forces' especially where classification models such as PESTEL are used. The concept of 'driving forces' is an artificially constructed one, constructed both to try to make sense of a changing world and to introduce order into the study of complexity. One can argue that the 'forces' do not exist in the real world. They are the product of reification. Certainly, models with various acronyms such as PESTEL may not provide a definitive classification of driving forces. Finally, providing a set of boxes to think within of itself constrains and limits thinking when the process is supposedly designed to break existing mental schema.

Rather than focusing upon abstract 'forces', we argue later that it is more useful to focus primarily on real human actors, those individuals who, in coalitions, are in positions of influence to redefine the world order.

There is a third issue, somewhat related to the first mentioned here – about the range of potential 'future shocks' that a business operating in a boundaryless, global world might experience. The early 1970s work conducted by Shell focused on the oil price, because at that time a price spike was the major shock that could impact the business significantly. Today, the number of vulnerable 'soft spots' in a global business has increased many fold and using the same old scenario approach the scenario team has to handle vastly more data points and complexity. In those days before the Internet and before the current foray towards globalisation, a few scenarios may have provided the foundation for organisational resilience. Now their capacity to do so is, somewhat, questionable.

The final problem relates to the question of who creates the scenarios. The author's experience of working with scenarios over the past two decades has shown that it is very difficult for observers, outside of the team that created the scenarios, to appreciate the underlying sense, logic and possibilities of the scenarios. It seems that being a part of the building process is really important for being able to understand the meaning of the future stories that emerge. It is probably in the process that the richness of the debate creates a really deep awareness of what words mean and what implications arise from various linkages between the stories and players within them. This complexity is hard to capture in a scenario story, or is somehow lost in the telling. Without an appreciation of this 'psychology', it is difficult to use them to full effect in a decision-making process.

The 'Universal Thought Space'

A rarely used, but potentially valuable approach to overcome these shortcomings is the development of a universal 'scenario space' or 'thought space'. This is of particular relevance in this world of potential catastrophic collapses and global complexity. A Universal Thought Space sets out in advance a broad range of unbounded futures.

A notable example of the application of this approach is the 'Trilemma Triangle' used by Shell to generate the Shell Global Scenarios to 2025 (Shell International 2005). This was designed to produce a foundation that would allow the construction of a far more comprehensive set of potential futures than could be achieved by using the more traditional approach described above. In short, it aimed to counter the limitations of reduction and scope that we referred to earlier. But, Shell's trilemma still used a variant of the concept of 'driving forces' discussed earlier.

The 'Trilemma Triangle' was arguably one of the first attempts to produce a Universal Thought Space that could be used as a foundation upon which to build answers to more focused scenario questions. This trilemma approach set out to prepare, for the organisation, a view of the range of all possible forms that the global environment could take. But before going further, it would be helpful to describe the 'trilemma concept'.

A trilemma is usually applied to a situation where a choice has to be made between three options, but it is only feasible to produce a compromise between two, not all three of the options. Two of the options can be made, with negotiation or adjustment, to work together, but getting a lasting compromise between all three is impossible. A simple and humorous example of a trilemma would be Zizek's Trilemma (Zizek 2007), where Zizek reflects that, in the Communist system, it was impossible to be simultaneously honest, to genuinely support communism and, at the same time, to be intelligent. 'If one was honest and supportive, one was not very bright; if one was bright and supportive, one was not honest; if one was honest and bright, one was not supportive.'

Shell's approach was influenced by 'Rodrik's Triangle' (Rodrik 2000). In this work, Rodrik was interested in the future course of globalisation, from the perspective of economic integration. This work has been further developed (Rodrik 2011) and Rodrik's Triangle or Trilemma consists of choices between:

(a) 'Hyper-globalisation' – this describes a fully integrated global economy where national borders ultimately become irrelevant. At an extreme we see all barriers to trade and the flow of capital removed. Individual countries have very little, if any, influence. In his earlier work, Rodrik also refers to this as an 'international economic integration'. The outcome of this force therefore is to create one global marketplace.
(b) Nation states – defined as 'territorial jurisdictional entities with independent powers of making and administering the law' (Rodrik 2000, p. 180). This force, unlike 'hyper-globalisation', values the power of national determination.
(c) 'Mass politics' (later renamed 'Democratic politics') – defined as 'political systems where: a) the franchise is unrestricted; b) there is a high degree of political mobilisation; and c) political institutions are responsive to mobilised groups' (Rodrik 2000, p. 180). Here, the emphasis is not on the state or the machinery of capitalism but on the role of democracy.

Rodrik's point is that it is impossible to satisfy all three at the same time. One cannot simultaneously respond to the demands of hyper-globalisation (effectively a world without borders), nation states and have locally representative democracies. There are only three compromises that Rodrik holds are viable, each being a compromise between two of the three choices mentioned above.

From this foundation, the Shell trilemma focused on three forces:

(1) market incentives – the 'pull' of global economic integration
(2) the force of the community – aspirations to social cohesion and justice
(3) coercion, regulation – or control as exercise by the state.

The approach to developing a universal scenario space described here differs from the above approaches in that the focus is not upon 'forces' but the behaviours of coalitions of critical actors who can influence the future world order. It is held that it is necessary to focus not on 'forces' but on the key actors or architects of the current and future world orders. Our interest is in human behaviour, not forces; we are interested in how the motivators and behaviours of key actors will change and evolve over time. As Gilpin (1981) notes:

> Strictly speaking, states, as such, have no interests, or what economists call 'utility functions', nor do bureaucracies, interest groups or so-called transnational actors for that matter. Only individuals and individuals joined together into various types of coalitions can be said to have interests.
>
> (Gilpin 1981, p. 18)

Whenever we talk of 'actors' we have in mind the individuals who form the guiding coalitions. These are the people who can attempt to change the world working in their coalitions or with other coalitions.

So, our challenge is to identify the actors, the coalitions of individuals, who are the current 'architects' of the world order. This challenge also extends to the consideration of whether or not new 'architects' could appear in the future.

In summary, the selection of critical actors has been influenced by Bull (1977), Bobbitt (2008), Friedrichs (2001), Harvey (2010) and Thomas (2000, 2005). These researchers identify coalitions who could play a central role in shaping a future order in a complex world, but have subtly different objectives and motivators. There are four coalitions that are identified, being 'state elites', 'market elites', 'social movements' and a new, emerging entity, that we will call the 'post-state elites'. Each will be introduced in turn.

(1) State elites. Currently, members of 'state elites' have access to the controls and coercive influence of the state. These actors can decide to what extent authority is centred in and exercised by the state. In other words, who is rewarded and who is punished. An extreme example of centralised control would be the planned economy of the Soviet Union. North Korea and the People's Republic of China also spring to mind as examples, in differing degrees, of the use of centralised decision-making and control. Autocracies, oligarchies and Fascist single-party systems all represent highly centralised systems of rule. Examples of the state elite in the UK and US would include Parliament and the House of Representatives, respectively. A more centralised example would be the Supreme Leader of Iran who has the authority both to declare war and over-ride elected bodies. These are the 'controllers' of territorially defined states.

(2) Market elites. Here we are concerned with key players in the market economy and their interests. These include multi-national corporations, investment banks, rating agencies and the wealthy individuals that Harvey (2010) sees as being major holders of influence. These actors, at an extreme, would want the total removal of all trade barriers and the minimisation of the role of the state or any successor to the state. This is free market capitalism, or neo-liberalism, where the market economy is allowed a free hand to allocate resources and, in extreme future forms, may even assume responsibility for the welfare of the individual.

(3) Social movements. Social movements embrace groups, even individuals in society whose values are of utmost importance to them. Adherence to these values or cultural norms is more important than allegiance to a territorially defined state or the accumulation of financial wealth. Examples of social movements range from environmentalists to potentially the most influential of all, religious groups. Social movements can pursue their aims using both peaceful and violent means. Some may have little interest in democracy or be opposed to the concept of democratic representation. It must be stressed that for members of social movements legitimacy emanates from beliefs, culture and values. For many in the world, values, historic cultures and beliefs assume far more

importance than the geographic boundaries of the state or the wealth generated by economic markets (Guzansky and Berti 2011).

Critically, social movements have been largely ignored in the international relations field (Thomas 2000), and we know too little about the role that they may have in reshaping our world.

(4) Post-state elites. An important, but potentially difficult, point to conceive is that we must not limit our thinking to a world of territorially defined states (although it is easiest to think this way as the world stands at the moment). The concept of the world as a system of states is a relatively new one and, in medieval times, there was less emphasis on territorial boundaries. Decisions were made by a dispersed group of appointed 'princes' (kings, dukes, counts, bishops and abbots), the nobility of the Holy Roman Empire and authority was delegated across this broad network. There are some, for example Bobbitt (2008), Bull (1977) and Friedrichs (2001), who feel that, under the pressure of demands for economic globalisation, the world could revert to this more 'virtual' and less territorially defined method of organising. We cannot discount the possibility that the states system could dissolve. The breakdown of the state and its replacement by, for example, networks of globally interlinked cities or 'mega states' is a topic that frequently arises during our scenario planning sessions at Cass when we consider the future of globalisation. Thinking should not therefore be bounded by the structure of today's world. In the words of Hedley Bull, 'states are simply groupings of men, and men may be grouped in such a way that they do not form states at all' (Bull 1977, p. 20). The European Union may be considered as a very early 'prototype'.

These, it is held, are the actors or, more correctly, architects of the future world.

Each of these four groups of actors can be positioned at four poles of the 'Universal Thought Space' as shown in Figure 3.1. The critical point is that each group of actors has very different objectives and motivators. State elites, at the extreme, want control over what happens at least within their own territorial domain of control. Market elites have different motivators. Again, at an extreme, market elites are not at all interested in borders; they see borders as blockages in the way of free trade. In their view, it is only a freely operating global economy that can efficiently allocate resources and generate wealth for all. Market

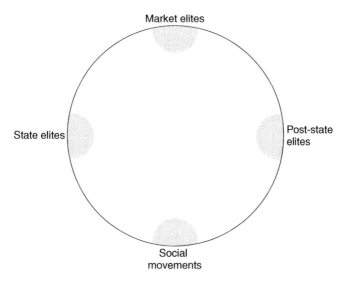

Market elites

State elites

Post-state
elites

Social
movements

Figure 3.1   The Universal Thought Space
Source: Davies (2012).

elites believe that they can make decisions faster and more effectively than elected governments (Altman 2011).

Social movements may not be interested in material wealth or state borders at all. Social movements are more concerned with wealth generation in terms of the values and behaviours that are their 'central life interests'. A large subset may be interested in pursuing democratic representation, but this will not be an objective for all social movements. Others may be totally opposed to democratic representation.

Looking to the future, post-state elites are concerned with control and influence that may not be limited to or defined by territorial boundaries.

It is impossible for the needs of all four groups of actors to be satisfied simultaneously for any length of time. It might be possible to satisfy the needs of more than two groups for a very short period of time, but the 'relationship' will quickly unravel as competing interests surface. It may also be possible, in the short to medium term, for one group to dominate and ignore the needs of other groups (as the Soviet Union attempted), but over time the attacks from other actors will be impossible to repel.

Following Friedrichs (2001), for a system to work and to provide relative stability in the long term, no one group of actors must dominate and that for stability to prevail a balance or 'constructive tension' must exist between two of the four actors. In practice, we hold that there is always one group that is more influential than the other when such a compromise or 'constructive tension' between two actors is formed.

From this basis, Davies (2012) presents a set of rules to be applied when using the thought space:

Rule 1: Compromise between all four groups of actors is impossible in anything more than the very short term. Conflicting views will rapidly unravel any agreement.

Rule 2: One group of actors can dominate and impose their way, but this will only exist in the short to medium term. It is impossible to resist the demands of the other groups of actors in the longer term. These shorter-term zones are shown in grey at each of the four poles of the thought space in Figure 3.1.

Rule 3: In a long-term compromise between two groups, there is a dominant group and an influential group that has a voice, but gives way voluntarily to the dominant group. It is impossible to reach a perfect power-sharing agreement between two groups. If we look at Figure 3.2 we can see these longer-term 'settling points' in the context of a world that is familiar to us now. At each 'settling point', there are two possible relationships, depending upon which group is dominant.

Rule 4: There will always be a dominant group and an influential group in any relationship. The dominant and, to a lesser degree, the influential group are the real architects. The voices of the other groups are heard, but their influence is limited and only passing attention is paid to them. We therefore have two long-term viable relationships between each pair of actors. These are shown by the darker grey segments, the 'settling points', in each relationship zone.

This approach produces a wider range of possible forms that the world order could take. The full range is presented in Figure 3.3.

At a first examination, this appears to be a complex bewildering picture, but it reflects the complexity of a future that the forces of globalisation may have unwittingly released. This approach does however produce a 'Universal Thought Space' that can be applied to provide the background context to any foresight exercise and, as we demonstrate

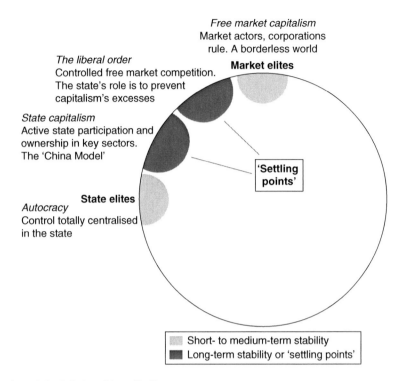

Figure 3.2   Relationships of influence
Source: Davies (2012).

below, it can be applied in a straightforward manner in any organisation. Table 3.1 provides a summary description of each of the 'setting points' shown in Figure 3.3.

If there is one lesson to take from the late 20th century, it is that it is highly unlikely that we will be faced with a quest for a single world order. We should think of a world of 'multiple orders'. The thought space can be used to consider how, over time, different orders will appear, co-exist or fade away.

The 'Universal Thought Space' is proposed as a new tool, like the others described in this book, in the armoury of the strategist. It sits alongside the traditional strategy and planning process with its focus on one future and one set of actions. It can also sit alongside established scenario methodologies which are, we hold, still valuable to explore specific, focused questions.

The purpose of the thought space is to provide a less bounded way of considering how the world could evolve. It is recommended for use

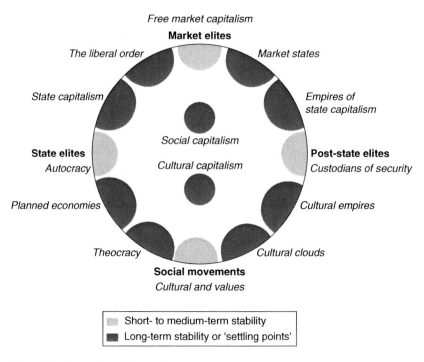

Figure 3.3   Potential relationships
Source: Davies (2012).

by the top-level decision-making team in the organisation. If the key decision-makers use it to consider future worlds, then they will not be gripped by the tyranny of the present. The organisation will be, as Shell was in respect of the oil crisis of the early 1970s, better prepared for a shift in power and influence than its competitors.

Key activities

There are five suggested key activities. Each activity has the objective of 'reducing the shock of the unknown' and should be completed by the top-level decision-making team. As we have observed earlier, without such involvement, it will be impossible for the team to grasp the underlying implications of each world in a unified manner.

The first task is to look out over the next 20 years. The task is to define the two key architects (from state elites, market elites, social movements and post-state elites) that will hold the highest positions of power and influence 20 years from now. The output of this first exercise

Table 3.1   Old and new relationships

Settling points	Relationship characteristics:
The liberal order	When looking at state elites and market elites there are two viable relationships to consider.
State capitalism	The first is the most familiar, which we can call *the liberal order*. The state elites maintain a degree influence and control, but market elites are the dominant party. It is interesting to note that the world order imposed after the Second World War tried to ensure a balance of influence between states and market elites. From the late 1970s, market elites assumed increasing power and we progressed towards a more extreme position where market elites would become the single dominant actor. Ultimately, this is a position of instability. The second is a position where the state is the dominant actor. We can call this *State Capitalism*. A current example is the 'Beijing Consensus'.
Social capitalism	The partners here are market elites and social movements. The influence of the state elites and any successor is insignificant.
Cultural capitalism	If market elites are the dominant party then we have the 'borderless world' referred to by Ohmae (1995). Territorial borders are dismantled in the interests of economic efficiency. The role of the state diminishes to such a degree that organisations take on many traditional functions of the state including the provision of welfare, healthcare and security. Social movements assume the regulatory role once undertaken by the state. We can call this position *Social Capitalism*. If social movements assume the dominant position, this is still a 'borderless world', but the interests of social movements dominate. This is a difficult place where the world may be divided not along territorial boundaries, but into more 'virtual layers', each layer controlled by one social movement (such as a religious order). Organisations will be tightly controlled by the beliefs of the relevant social movement. Here, organisations are regulated by social movements, not the state. Working across 'virtual layers' will present new challenges for many organisations. This may well not be a totally democratic world. We can call this *Cultural Capitalism*.
Theocracy	The partnership here is between state elites and social movements, again a totally new relationship.
Planned economies	If social movements assume the upper hand, then world of territorial borders reappears. Capitalism may well exist but is potentially tightly regulated primarily by social movements. This is a world divided by culture and beliefs.

Table 3.1   (Continued)

Settling points	Relationship characteristics:
	The generation of material wealth may take third place behind culture, beliefs and the demands of the state elites. This relationship can be referred to as *Theocracy*.
	When state elites assume the dominant role, we can reach the position where capitalism becomes extinguished and is replaced by centralised control. The planned economies of the Soviet era are an ideological example. This is a world where the credibility of the market elites has been destroyed, wealth, materialism and consumerism are all eschewed. Stability, security and culture are valued far more than material wealth. This is a world of *planned economies*.
Market states	This is a world where territorially bound states fade into history, unable to cope with the ravages of globalisation. The most likely successor is a 'super state' or a collection of ideologically aligned former states. An alternative is a world where power is ceded to networks of cities that become the focal points for economic growth.
Empires of state capitalism	If market elites are the most influential we have the emergence of the *Market States* that Bobbitt (2008) describes.
	But if influence is centred upon the post-state elite, we have large aggregations appearing where capitalism is valued, but not before control and security. We could call these the *Empires of State Capitalism*.
Cultural clouds	Our final zone may be the most difficult for those of us who have grown up in a consumer society to conceive.
Cultural empires	If social movements take a dominant position we have the possibility of vast areas of cultural influence that penetrate all physical borders. This is a very difficult world for organisations. They will have little influence and may have to align with a specific social movement to survive. We could call this world *Cultural Clouds*.
	If the post-elites take the upper hand we have a world of vast ideologically aligned blocs, where wealth and profit take third place behind culture, values and security. This is a world of *Cultural Empires*.

will tell us the range of future worlds that we have to explore in more detail. If we were to conclude that market elites and post-state elites will be the most influential, then our 'zone of exploration' runs clock-wise from '*Free Market Capitalism*' to '*Custodians of Security*' in Figure 3.3.

The second task is to develop pictures or descriptions of these four future worlds.

The third activity is the definition of a series of response strategies. The objective is to define how the organisation will react if faced by the emergence of a particular new world. The key issues to be addressed obviously include selection of target markets and offerings. But arguably the most important focal points include the impact on the organisation in terms of its culture, structure and competences. Using these findings, the team can define in advance how change within the organisation will be managed. This is more than an attractive academic exercise. If we are to learn lessons both from the fall of the Soviet Union and the Arab Spring of 2011, then it is that change in the world can occur quickly and rapidly. Possibly we do not live in a world of slow, incremental change, but in a world of 'the punctuated equilibrium' or Ferguson's 'catastrophic collapses'. Advance preparation is a luxury that the thought space can provide us with.

The fourth activity is to identify the potential pathways of change. Where will we move to from the present? How will power and influence be transferred? The broad consensus before the *Great Recession* was that a future world would take on the form and values of the liberal order. The influential actors would be the market elites of the financial markets. Even China, it was thought, when it enjoyed the fruits of capitalism, would gradually liberalise to join other advanced nations in the realm of the liberal order. The task now is to define future potential pathways of change, in which direction are we headed and what will be the characteristics of change? Will we be faced with slow, evolutionary change or the more violent environment of the punctuated equilibrium and the catastrophic collapse? Who will be the masters of the future world? Will we move not from one world order to another, but from one dominant order to multiple orders?

The fifth and final role for the thought space is to act as a framework to make sense of current events. Without such a framework it is difficult to piece together disparate events as they appear. Considering such events within the domain of the Universal Thought Space can help us to see how power and influence is shifting between the four groups of architects and in what direction the world order is headed.

There is still a role for conventional scenario planning that has proven itself to be a valuable tool to help manage uncertainties, but we would argue that another tool is now required to sit alongside it.

We need to be sure that we can survive the catastrophe of the unexpected.

References

Altman, R. (2011). *We Need not Fret Over Omnipotent Markets*. FT.com. Available at: http://www.ft.com/cms/s/0/890161ac-1b69-11e1-85f8-00144feabdc0.html#axzz1fHKcTLBn [Accessed December 2, 2011].

Bobbitt, P. (2008). *Terror and Consent: The Wars for the Twenty-First Century*, London: Penguin.

Bull, H. (1977). *The Anarchical Society: A Study of Order in World Politics* 2nd ed., Houndmills: Macmillan.

Davies, R.D. (2012). *The Era of Global Transition*, Houndmills: Palgrave Macmillan.

Ferguson, N. (2010). Complexity and Collapse. *Foreign Affairs* 89(2): 18–32.

Friedrichs, J. (2001). The Meaning of New Medievalism. *European Journal of International Relations* 7(4): 475–502.

Gilpin, R. (1981). *War and Change in World Politics*, Cambridge: Cambridge University Press.

Guzansky, Y. and Berti, B. (2011). *The Arab Spring's Violent Turn*. The National Interest. Available at: http://nationalinterest.org/commentary/the-arab-springs-violent-turn-6254 [Accessed December 16, 2011].

Harvey, D. (2010). *The Enigma of Capital and the Crises of Capitalism*, London: Profile Books.

Ohmae, K. (1995). *The End of the Nation State: The Rise of the Regional Economies*, London: Harper Collins.

Ralston, B. and Wilson, I. (2006). *The Scenario Planning Handbook: A Practitioner's Guide to Using Scenarios to Direct Strategy in Today's Uncertain Times*, Ohio: Thomson.

Ranson, S., Hinings, B. and Greenwood, R. (1980). The Structuring of Organizational Structures. *Administrative Science Quarterly* 25(1): 1–17.

Rodrik, D. (2000). How Far Will International Economic Integration Go? *Journal of Economic Perspectives* 14(1): 177–186.

Rodrik, D. (2011). *The Globalization Paradox: Why Global Markets, States and Democracy Can't Coexist*, Oxford: Oxford University Press.

Schwartz, P. (2009). *Your Future in 5 Easy Steps: Wired Guide to Personal Scenario Planning*. Wired. Available at: http://www.wired.com/special_multimedia/2009/ff_scenario_1708 [Accessed February 4, 2012].

Shell International (2005). *The Shell Global Scenarios to 2025 – The Future Business Environment: Trends, Trade-offs and Choices*, London: Shell.

Thomas, S. (2000). Taking Religious and Cultural Pluralism Seriously: The Global Resurgence of Religion and the Transformation of International Society. *Millennium: Journal of International Studies* 29(3): 815–841.

Thomas, S. (2005). *The Global Resurgence of Religion and the Transformation of International Relations*, New York: Palgrave Macmillan.

Verity, J. (2003). Scenario Planning as a Strategy Technique. *European Business Journal* 14(4): 185–195.

Wack, P. (1985). The Gentle Art of Reperceiving. Scenarios, Uncharted Waters Ahead. *Harvard Business Review* September/October: 73–89; and Scenarios, Shooting the Rapids. *Harvard Business Review* November/December: 139–150.
Weick, K. (1995). *Sensemaking in Organisations*, Thousand Oaks: Sage.
Wilkinson, L. (2009). *How to Build Scenarios*. Wired. Available at: http://www. wired.com/wired/scenarios/build.html [Accessed February 4, 2012].
Zizek, S. (2007). *The Dreams of Others*. These Times. Available at: http://www. inthesetimes.com/the_dreams_of_others/ [Accessed January 25, 2012].

4
Design Thinking

Julie Verity and Kevin McCullagh

Reviving an old process for a new need?

In 2006, Tim Brown was invited to the World Economic Forum in Davos. The Forum has an ambitious agenda, which is a commitment 'to improving the state of the world by engaging business, political, academic and other leaders of society to shape global, regional and industry agendas' (www.weforum.org). So why is it interesting that Tim Brown was an invitee to this assembly of the World's leadership cadre? The answer lies in his background and the work he currently does at the rapidly growing consultancy, IDEO. Educated at Newcastle Polytechnic (as it was then known) and the Royal College of Art in the UK, he is an industrial designer. He has won awards for work exhibited at the Museum of Modern Art in New York and the Design Museum in London. He is the Chief Executive Officer (CEO) and President of IDEO which is a global design consultancy.

Since the millennium, the profile of design among leaders of businesses, organisations, government offices and NGOs has been elevated to a status that it probably has never achieved before, and Brown and IDEO have ridden the crest of this popular wave ahead of many of the other renowned designers and design houses.

Why now? And what has this to do with strategy?

The IDEO website states: 'IDEO helps companies build businesses, innovate, develop capabilities and grow', all of which sounds strategic. And it doesn't stop at business. IDEO also consult for governments, and Brown makes speeches about what design thinking can do for nations (Brown 2010). Designers have become strategists and strategy consultants to the world's largest organisations and communities. Just a decade ago, this was not so. Then, design input to strategy would more likely have been about putting the glossy cover on the final document. Now, the way designers are educated to think is seen to be particularly relevant, and not just to add attractive exteriors to products, services and brands, but as a way to create completely new value, to be strategic and solve the most complex organisational problems.

This chapter explores what the current fascination with design is and whether what has become known as *Design Thinking* adds to strategic thinking. Popularity suggests there is substance in the design approach but is it, as one of the founders of IDEO said, 'a new story, not a new process' (McCullagh 2010), and even if this is the case, is it an old process whose time has come (again)?

Defining design thinking

So, how do designers think? What is the magic that is learnt at a design school rather than in an economics class or in management? First, Brown (2010) states that designing is a craft:

> As a designer I ply my craft in the turbulent waters between the complex things we create and the human beings they are intended to serve. Often I define design as getting the interface right between technology and people. If you accept... [that] technology means all manmade things including business and political systems. Therefore design can be about getting the interface right between businesses and people, politics and people or gadgets and people.

Second, it is a completely different way of thinking compared with critical thinking, a distinction Simon (1969) made over 40 years ago:

> ... [defining] 'design' as the 'transformation of existing conditions into preferred ones' Design Thinking is, then, always linked to an improved future. Unlike critical thinking, which is a process of analysis and is associated with the 'breaking down' of ideas, design thinking is a creative process based around the 'building up' of ideas. There are no judgments in design thinking. This eliminates the fear of failure and encourages maximum input and participation. Wild ideas are welcome, since these often lead to the most

creative solutions. Everyone is a designer, and design thinking is a way to apply design methodologies to any of life's situations.

In Simon's definition, we find more characteristics about design thinking: that creativity is fundamental, that participation is encouraged, that failure is acceptable and that the purpose is to enhance humanity.

There is much shared ground between this concept of the designers' skills and those associated with 'right brain thinking'. Pink (2005) describes these as: 'the ability to see patterns and opportunities, to create artistic and emotional beauty, to craft a satisfying narrative and to combine seemingly unrelated ideas into something new...[combined with]...the ability to empathise with others, to understand the subtleties of human interaction,...to stretch beyond the quotidian in pursuit of purpose and meaning'. Pink is no less ambitious about the potential of design thinking than his fellow advocates. If it is widely adopted, he contends, it can be put to its ultimate purpose of changing the world (p. 70).

Verganti (2006), after studying a group of highly innovative, Milan-based manufacturers, concluded that while not all designed products changed the lives of their users for the better, there were design-driven innovation *processes* that could produce products with breakthrough potential. These products, he argued, commanded higher margins for longer, compared with products where designers were complying with the industry norm of adding the 'final flourish'. In line with Simon's assertion that designing is at the command of everyone, Verganti also found that training as an artist or designer was not required to create such a process, but being able to collaborate with artists, scientists, craftsmen and chief executives was required to make products that *'consumers find delightful, meaningful, and worthy of their loyalty'*.

In this work, Verganti ties design with sustainable profit and a design-led process with breakthrough ideas and long-term value creation. However, whilst Verganti is a designer, he actively distances himself from the 'design thinking' term and field.

A different path to a definition

Slightly ahead of the wave of popularity of understanding designers' minds and processes, Martin and Austen (1999) questioned the way leaders of 21st-century organisations needed to think. They proposed that the new millennium would be typified by constant change and relentless competition and for this climate management would succeed by practising the *Art of Integrative Thinking*. There are no references to design here, but there are many to artistry, complex problem solving, continual learning, surprising new ideas and creativity which are all needed in large quantity.

Roger Martin is not a designer. He is an academic and was once head of Monitor, Michael Porter's strategy consultancy. He started using the language of design in 2004 in his paper – 'The Design of Business' – where he argued that the thought processes of business leaders needed to shift radically away from analytical reasoning to 'design sensibilities' in order to create value that was relevant in the new millennium (Martin 2004). His thesis, which he developed further in his book, was that the world is populated with *mysteries*, phenomena that we observe but do not understand. We are curious about these mysteries and probe into them, exploring hunches about ways to solve them. This leads to experimentation and simplification, ways to put solutions into action, and soon they become what Martin calls *heuristics*. In the business world these are fledgling entrepreneurial companies, new products, innovative services or new process solutions. Over time and with repeated practice, trial and error and learning, heuristics can be converted into *algorithms*. These are reliable, scalable business models that deliver on the brand promise in a known and predictable way. Repeating the algorithm delivers efficiency and drives profitability. Inevitably the algorithm can be converted to simple code and be copied or replicated, but this is all code can do. Code cannot innovate or solve new mysteries.

The case example is McDonalds. Back in the 1950s, the mystery the McDonald brothers probed was what Californians wanted to eat on their drive home from the beach. The heuristic which solved the problem was fast-food restaurants serving a limited menu. It was successful and became a phenomenal global success over the subsequent decades when Ray Kroc refined and honed the heuristic into an algorithm: an operating specification that was 99.9% repeatable and predictable everywhere. Martin argues that this route to value creation was the pattern for much of the 20th century throughout Western businesses.

As with most success stories, however, at some point they turn sour and in the 1990s McDonalds lost part of the fast-food market to Subway, a company that offered customers fast-food which met their new desires of a healthier diet. Martin (2009) contends that the management at McDonalds were stuck in their own algorithm. They had lost the ability to revisit the mystery of 'what people wanted to eat' 50 years on and to explore it anew for changes and fresh angles. Unlike Subway's leaders who had capitalised on the mystery by doing the very thinking McDonalds had lost their appetite for (!)

Martin proposed that different types of thinking are required in different measure at different points in the mystery-to-code process. When solving mysteries, intuitive thinking is required in a process of exploration and discovery. This sort of thinking is about looking for the extraordinary, the unexpected and trying to imagine what might be. Whereas, creating algorithms from heuristics requires what Ray Kroc was expert at and what Martin suggests is analytical reasoning. McDonalds were stuck in analytical logic and an increasingly intense requirement from the hierarchy to prove that a change in the business model would result in desired outcomes. Proof by measurement, proof by previous experience or proof by projection of past success, business cases for the future needed to carry a weight of logic and numbers and sound analytics.

Using this metaphor of how businesses capture and harvest value over time and the different thinking processes that are required to deliver value over the business cycle – ranging from exploration (intuitive thinking) to exploitation (analytical thinking) – Martin argues that both are required for 21st-century value creation. Where businesses are stuck in the heuristic phase, they are missing out on the efficiency gains they could make by creating algorithmic knowledge inside the business. Where businesses are stuck in the algorithm, or worse with fully codified internal systems, intuitive thinking is required to stimulate innovation. Since Martin's thesis is that many western businesses are in this latter category, the cure is to restore the balance of thinking so that companies can do both – explore and exploit. And this is how Martin defines design thinking, as this harmonious sharing of mind-space between the intuitive and analytical.

A balance of two minds

Martin's thesis did not start with designers' talents or skills in mind, and he has joked that he should find a better name for his concept which probably gives too much credence to designers' ability to be analytical (McCullagh 2010). However, he is not alone in his analysis about the last century. Pink (2005) confers that 'for nearly a Century, Western society in general, and American society in particular, has been dominated by a form of thinking and an approach to life that is narrowly reductive and deeply analytical'. And in his reflection on the evolution of design thinking, Vogel (2009) looks further back and argues that it was John Ruskin and William Morris who started a movement against what they saw to be the industrial revolution gone too far at the end of the 19th century. Out of their criticism of the standardisation, mass-manufactured goods and services and 'quantitative management' of the era arose the Arts and Crafts movement where designers and architects rebelled against the inhuman scale, scientific nature of the production line and its utilitarian outputs. Vogel argues that, with some notable exceptions, the schism between these two philosophies persisted throughout the last century and that the current notion of design thinking is an attempt at bringing these two opposing approaches of technology and craft together.

We can conclude that everything is designed. Even utilitarian objects created in a standardised format emanating from the end of a production line have been designed. But that this is not what is meant by 'design sensibilities'. Everyone can be a designer but not everyone is trained, or is predisposed, to engage the right-hand side of their brain. Design is about creativity *more* than it is about analytical rigour, but contemporary design thinking is evolving into a synthesis of creative *and* scientific approaches to problem solving. It is about 'being' in *both* the natural environment and the man-made world. It employs human intuition *and* analytical reasoning – a balance of two minds. It takes account of context and time in terms of life-cycle thinking. It embraces complexity in a holistic way and provides elegant solutions that resolve conflicts. The aim is to make life better for people – mostly consumers and communities.

How to do it

Brown (2009) describes the IDEO process in some detail. He starts by prescribing a mixed team of professionals, consumers, stakeholders and experts from the wider world. He splits the process into three 'spaces of innovation': inspiration, ideation and implementation, also stressing that this is a circular and iterative process.

On the BBC radio 4 *In Business* programme (2009), Brown described this process and highlighted where design thinking differed from typical business analysis:

Inspiration

  (i) designers get inspired by people
  (ii) designers don't do benchmarking or analysis of the current business
  (iii) they get involved in the user experience and search for the things that are often *not* articulated
  (iv) designers observe closely and keep users and potential consumers involved, they 'live' the problem
  (v) designers struggle with the initial problem and try to resolve what the fundamental question behind the problem is without closing it down too early or taking it at face value.

In this space: (Inspiration), the tools the designer might reach for are: storytelling and role playing. The skills are watching, listening and empathy. The physical place is also important, it creates the atmosphere for intuitive thinking (Brown 2008, ABC Nightline 2009) and the team needs to get out into the world and experience the strategic problem in context, actively exploring potential solutions.

The message of this space is that inspiration doesn't come from a second-hand experience at the desk.

Ideation

  (i) this space is for exploration
  (ii) typically traditional business problem-solvers would already be converging on an idea
  (iii) but, designers keep open minds, searching for ideas that *have not been thought of before*
  (iv) designers search for many ideas accepting that any proposition can be improved, refined or bring something to the party. Even proposals that go nowhere can add value purely because of the discussion and learning that is involved in rejecting them.

Inside the ideation space, the tools required are brainstorming, sketching-out ideas, storyboards and storytelling, building scenarios, building prototypes and testing, testing, testing. The skill is to risk failure early and often, to involve all the capabilities that are available (including customers and people within the business).

Ideation is not about choosing and rejecting (which is often what strategic choice forces on us) or copycatting (benchmarking against competitors), but about building-up ideas into breakthrough concepts.

Implementation

(i) selling the idea into the organisation
(ii) this is not *just* about a written business proposal in a formal document
(iii) bring the experience of the solution to the decision-makers.

Implementation is hard. Marketing skills involving building compelling stories, creating metaphors and images and communicating with impact are important in this phase.

Codified thinking – *not!*

However, codifying the process into steps does not describe the craft. After 'living' the process at the Aspen Design Summit in 2010, Helen Walters, the former editor of innovation and design at *Business Week*, titled her article on design thinking an 'Opaque Process': '*Those looking for a prescribed way to implement design thinking are destined to be disappointed. It's a messy, opaque process that depends as much on group dynamics as intellect or insight*' (Walters 2009). Judging by her final sentence, however, the messiness was worth it: 'The ... [experience] ... provided a compelling case study on the potential of design thinking, a provocative, compelling and often messy process that keeps those involved up at night – and might just help change the world, community by community'.

And this could be a major problem for the future of design thinking. Most writers do describe the technique as a step-wise process. Beckman and Barry (2007) have four steps in the innovation process, but they do argue that this is not easy to implement, that *it is not meant to be implemented in rote fashion*. The art of mastering the process for Beckman and Barry is twofold. The first is balancing the team of people involved in multiple dimensions, different disciplinary fields and representation from different learning styles. The second is ensuring that no step in the process is missed or given short-change. Their experience is that a diverse team will necessitate careful management due to the conflicts of style and approach that are inherent, and that many organisations lean towards either existing in the concrete sphere of learning or entirely in the abstract, resulting in valuable steps being ignored.

Martin and Austen's (1999) *integrative* thought process also offers a four-step process. But again, this process is not linear, instead it requires judgement and practice. The authors stress that even when it is explained, it is hard to know how to do it, suggesting a rich content of tacit knowledge.

So, while design thinking can be articulated and codified into phases, what this process is and where one phase begins and another finishes is complex. Verganti (2009) argues that this is as it should be. He makes the argument for keeping the process broad, flexible according to the context and wide open to the introduction of new ideas, thus keeping it alive and able to evolve.

The very idea that design thinking could be learnt by the corporate suits from process descriptions is what prompted Bruce Nussbaum to write in fastcodesign.com (2011):

> From the beginning, the process of Design Thinking was a scaffolding for the real deliverable: creativity. But in order to appeal to the business culture of process, it was denuded of the mess, the conflict, failure, emotions, and looping circularity that is part and parcel of the creative process. In a few companies, CEOs and managers accepted that mess along with the process and real innovation took place. In most others, it did not.

Nussbaum does not dispute the usefulness of the 'real' design thinking, in fact he goes on to announce the forthcoming publication of his own *new improved* version: CQ – Creative Intelligence, which he defines as: 'It is a sociological approach in which creativity emerges from group activity, not a psychological approach of development stages and individual genius'.

Hence, if design thinking is to continue to thrive and find life-improving, meaningful solutions, it must retain the messy, tacit humanness that results from people with a rich mix of skills, experiences and mindsets working together in conducive environments for as Dziersk (2008) eloquently put it: *a warm embrace of risk and new ideas.* Steve Jobs is reported to have said that those new ideas come from 'people meeting up in the hallways or calling each other at 10.30 at night with a new idea, or because they realized something that shoots holes in how we've been thinking about a problem. Its ad hoc meetings of six people called by someone who thinks he has figured out the coolest new thing ever and who wants to know what other people think of his idea' (Levy 2007).

Tom Peters once famously said that no great ideas come out of planning processes. What talented designers might add to these typically formal, mechanical, linear, box-filling, often hierarchical and numbers-based planning processes is well developed right-brain thinking skills, and the ability to create atmosphere and attitude that promotes bold, creative ideas and solutions. From the sentiment behind Jobs' words there is also the sense that people need to be engaged emotionally and strive with a sense of pride, rather than for financial reward, and to be tenacious in the pursuit of an elegant, original solution.

The table below attempts a summary of the differences between a design-thinking process and how we observe strategy typically happening today:

Design thinking		Common practice
Iterative, explorative, accepting of failure en-route, [faster?]	Process	Sequential [slower?]
Intimate primary research, close observation	Data	Secondary/desk data, quantitative, practitioner knowledge
Diverse expertise, balanced minds/disciplines	Who	C-suite, economists, analysts
Creative physical space, drawing, scribbling, building	How	Offices and away-days, power-point slides and figures
Creative leaps to deliver elegant, new-to-the-world solutions	Outcomes	Greater efficiency, incremental change
Today's problems – for tomorrow	Context	Predicting futures to move into
Tested prototype	Create	Written-down plan
Persuasive presentation, impactful, co-creation	Implement	Cascading/telling through the hierarchy
Curiosity, meaning and imagination	Under-pinning	Logic, figures, hard data
Improving people's lives	Purpose	Delivering shareholder value

Is design thinking the new competitive advantage?

Designers have been offering business solutions for centuries, even those that balance technology with craft. Vogel (2009) argues that this is what architect Peter Behrens was asked to do by AEG (the German electric company) in 1907. The brief was to help the company introduce the potential of electricity to consumers and that in achieving this task, Behrens succeeded in 'marrying the sophistication and human scale of craft heritage in European products with the emerging massive systems of electrical power generation and distribution'.

Examples of companies that use design to gain competitive advantage are not hard to find. Apple has already been mentioned and we could add to this Ferrari, Audi and Alessi whose iconic cars and household wares are not out of place in art galleries. These products deliver superior margins over longer periods of time compared with competitors. Verganti (2006) illustrates this and takes the example of model 9093 from the Alessi stable to provide a classic case study. This kettle, designed by Michael Graves and first retailed 26 years ago, still commands a premium price and position, both on retailers' shelves and in customers' hearts. If you are unfamiliar with model 9093, its spark of genius is a small coloured bird on the spout of the kettle which sings when the water boils. Apart from being functional, with a distinctive and beautiful body shape, the singing bird brings an extra dimension to this kettle which turns the ordinary, everyday activity of making tea into a joy. Verganti cites the story of a poet who sent Graves a postcard about the kettle: 'I am always grumpy when I get up in the morning. But when I get up now, I put the kettle on and when it starts to sing it makes me smile – goddamn you!'

This is competitive advantage gained from the application of a trained mind and talented craftsmanship to an everyday problem – of how to boil water – *and* add something more. Strategically this is not new, rather it is an example of Porterean generic differentiation par excellence. Design thinking does, however, revive the idea of innovating through creativity and meaningful added-value.

The classic design of an Audi TT is married with cutting-edge technologies (like voice control and direct-shift gear box) *and* elements that are algorithmic, like floor-pans which are common across other Audi and VW car models. The Audi brands provide an example nearer to the strategic practice Martin (2009) defines as design thinking. Designers work closely with engineers and brand managers, focusing on continual innovation in each area and adding low-cost solutions where the customer is unaware or doesn't care about it being undifferentiated. Whilst essentially a utilitarian product, the beauty and cleverness of the solutions Audi brings to its cars create emotional attachment, customer loyalty and a willingness to pay a higher price. As with Alessi's model 9093, however, there is little here that traditional strategy thinking could not have prompted if leadership was focused on constant innovation and integrated activity across the strategic strengths of the organisation.

So why is it high profile now?

Apple might be part of the answer. It is hard to say the word design and *not* automatically think Steve Jobs. Jobs returned to Apple in 1998, since when the company has become the totemic case study of how to out-innovate the competition through smart design. The days of putting the case for the importance of design were replaced by CEOs wanting to be the Apple of their industry.

Then there is the design-led rejuvenation of Procter and Gamble (P&G) (Martin 2009). One of Wall Street's benchmark companies of global proportions (at around $40 bn revenue), Martin describes an organisation in crisis when, in 2000 P&G made two profit warnings: share value dropped from $116 in January to around $60 in the summer and the top man in the C suite was asked to leave. This crisis came after a decade of restructuring and as a shock to the 165-year-old organisation.

Lafley, the replacement CEO, is the man attributed with turnaround success. Within three years, P&G was reporting profit growth of 15% pa and 13 of the company's top 15 brands had increased market shares. After acquiring and integrating Gillette, in 2006 P&G reported revenue growth of 10% pa, a fall in R&D costs from 4.8% to 3.6% of sales and 35% of their new product ideas coming from outside collaborators.

Martin's story about P&G fits his own model of design thinking. The turnaround success *is* explained by creating the role of chief innovation officer, changing market research methods, employing and integrating talented designers into the new product development processes, using design thinking protocols to solve problems almost everywhere in the organisation and training employees in the process. But Lafley also addressed costs, converting more of the organisation's *heuristics* to *algorithms* and cutting the internal R&D function to its core capability and supplementing this by using external collaborators; that is he applied his analytical thinking skills. Finally, he role-modelled a change in behaviour himself and aligned board-level and senior executive procedures to change fundamentally the culture of P&G.

We are not given a comparison with the P&G restructuring efforts of the nineties and why these failed, but we might surmise that design thinking provided an idea and a process with which to change what P&G valued and believed in and therefore how it behaved, which the mechanical restructuring of people within functions during the previous 10 years did not achieve.

So, there is evidence that designing solutions to complex problems works at a time when businesses and governments have fresh in their minds the costly failures of more 'scientific', bureaucratic processes of the past decade. For example, when IDEO were asked to help the Social Security Administration in the US to reduce costs, they impressed with a process that surprised civil servants because it was so: collaborative; observant of the final user; engaging; cut across their hierarchies; created energy and delivered bold prototype solutions with amazing speed (Metropolis 2011).

Speed is attractive. The iterative process that builds-in multiple perspectives in an intense period of interaction, together with the early introduction of prototyping, testing and failing, appears to deliver solutions faster and ones that are robust and likely to be implemented effectively. Given that designed solutions promise to be more original and differentiated, competitive advantage is likely to be sustained for longer. Speed could also mean lower cost.

Balanced thinking

Whatever we want to call it, design thinking meets a post-crisis, 21st-century need for more balanced thinking. The essence of the language, the process and the philosophy is that different minds and diverse personalities and skillsets, collaborating equally and equitably, improve strategic thinking. We might have always known this, but strategic practice has become quite different from this prescription in many organisations. The design-thinking approach to strategy emphasises the social nature of problem solving and the human element that economic-based practices tend to deny.

Inherent in the approach is the warning not to exclude analytical reasoning and tip the scales to the creative, intuitive extreme. One of the reasons we might fear this will happen is our self-knowledge and the recognition that we have a preference for relatively simple ways to think and for working with people who make sense of the world and work the same way as we do. As Beckman and Barry (2007) warn, one of the most difficult aspects of the process is to create a team discipline that allows diverse minds to work together.

This has to be managed through the leadership and culture of the organisation. Leaders need to understand and be able to manage the paradox of standardising and systemising parts of their operations while nurturing innovative, creative environments nearby. Cultures that foster co-existence of these extremes are relatively rare, but not unknown. Audi is cited above. Martin (2009) also cites several examples, including P&G after Lafley had introduced design-led processes. Martin argued that Lafley did not have a designer's skillset and therefore could not be the chief innovation officer himself, but he could embed the process into the culture and turn the process into a fruitful routine.

A second differentiating characteristic of this perspective over economic-based views is the notion that the meaning behind the endeavour of solving complex problems is to improve the human condition and our lives – not only with beautiful, new-to-the-world outcomes, but also by finding meaning in, and enjoying doing, the work itself. While the ultimate aim of capitalism and competitive strategy might also be life enhancement, the mantra of profit, superior rent generation and maximisation of shareholder value have substantially downgraded notions of deeper meaning. Tipping the balance excessively towards rational, financial, figure-based cultures encourages traits from the dark side of human nature – like selfishness, status-seeking and greed – to flourish. If design thinking does encourage double or triple bottom-line thinking (rather than shareholder value *only*), it has already been of great service in helping to shift mind-sets towards more sustainable and holistic ideas about the purpose of organisations.

Another positive outcome of the popularity of design thinking and its new intimacy with strategy is the focus it brings on innovation. While design thinkers cannot claim any glory for awareness of the need to be more innovative (it is more likely that environmental uncertainty explains this), the legitimisation of seeking entirely new solutions and bringing siloed disciplines together to create something 'strategic' is a shift in mindset. In many organisations, 'innovation' is often ring-fenced in skunk works, incubators and research labs and kept well away from corporate strategists. The journey from these hot-houses of ideas into the organisation's strategic future can often become a tortuous terrain littered with former great ideas.

There are also dangers ahead for design thinking. After such a speedy rise up corporate horizons, cracks are being highlighted that need fixing if it is to sustain and build its own reputation as a strategic device. These hone-in on the essentials described above, where top teams are turning the handle of a process that has ironed-out the creative tensions that occur between diverse teams of right- and left-brain thinkers – and are disappointed with the results and proclaiming it a fraud. Already, design thinking is in danger of being labelled 'fluff' and being challenged to find ways to articulate its value (Walters 2011, Nussbaum 2011).

In conclusion, design thinking is an old process that could be a new story:

1. Designers and business working together is a long-established practice.
2. Design thinking has gained popularity over the last decade as a way to tackle more complex problems including those we might label 'strategic'.
3. The elevation of design thinking to the strategic level is welcomed because it broadens current practice of strategic thinking and provides a richer seam of ideas to access.
4. Following Martin's (2009) formula, it emphasises the need for organisations to do *both*; explore and exploit simultaneously and continuously.
5. The process is not strongly prescribed and this should be seen as a strength, not a weakness, leaving it open to fit the context of the problem and for leaders to take responsibility for its development.
6. The adoption of 'design thinking' has delivered successes.
7. Compared with current/past practice, design thinking demands a more balanced approach to strategy by raising the necessity of 'right-brain' thinking and celebration of the human side of management and problem solving.

8. The ultimate aim of finding a 'designed' solution to a problem is to improve peoples' lives; this gives strategy a worthwhile and meaningful human community purpose, which is more motivating and *balanced* compared with the single, financial goal of shareholder value.

References

ABC Nightline (2009). Available at: www.youtube.com/watch?v= M66ZU2 PCIcM.

BBC Radio 4 (2009). *Grand Design*. Available at: http://www.bbc.co.uk/ programmes/b00jv9n0 [Accessed September 1, 2011].

Beckman, S. and Barry, M. (2007). Innovation as a Learning Process: Embedding Design Thinking. *California Management Review* 50(1), Fall: 25–56.

Brown, T. (2008). *Creativity and Play*. Available at: http://www.ted.com/talks/ lang/eng/tim_brown_on_creativity_and_play.html.

Brown, T. (2008a). Design Thinking. *Harvard Business Review* 86(6): 84–92.

Brown, T. (2009). *Change by Design; How Design Thinking Transforms Organisations and Inspires Innovation*, Boston: Harvard Business Press.

Brown, T. (2010). *Design Nations*. Available at: http://www.ideo.com [Accessed 08.2011].

Brown, T. (2011). *Davos Posts*. Available at: http://www.designthinking.com [Accessed 08.2011].

Dziersk, M. (2008). *Design Thinking. What is that?* Fast Company.com, July 8th. Available at: http://www.fastcompany.com/resources/design/dziersk/design-thinking-083107.html.

Esslinger, H. (2009). *A Fine Line: How Design Strategies are Shaping the Future of Business*, San Francisco: Jossey-Bass.

Kolb, D.A. (1984). *Experiential Learning: Experience as the Source of Learning and Development*, New Jersey: Prentice Hall.

Levy, S. (2007). *The Perfect Thing; How the iPod Shuffles Commerce, Culture and Coolness*, New York: Simon and Shuster.

Martin, R. (2004). The Design of Business. *Rotman Management* Winter: 7–11.

Martin, R. (2009). *The Design of Business: Why Design Thinking Is the Next Competitive Advantage*, Boston: Harvard Business Press.

Martin, R. and Austen, H. (1999). The Art of Integrative Thinking. *Rotman Management* Fall: 4–7.

McCullagh, K. (2010). Stepping up: Design Thinking has Uncovered Real Opportunities. *Design Management Review* 21(3): 36–39.

Metropolis (2011). *IDEO Takes on the Government*. Available at: http://www. metropolismag.com/story/20110609/ideo-takes-on-the-government.

Nussbaum, B. (2011). *Design Thinking is a Failed Experiment, So What's Next?* Available at: http://www.fastcodesign.com/1663558/design-thinking-is-a-failed-experiment-so-whats-next.

Pink, D.H. (2005). *A Whole New Mind – Moving from the Information Age to the Conceptual Age*, New York: Riverhead Books (Penguin Group).

Pisano, G.P. and Verganti, R. (2008). Which Kind of Collaboration Is Right for You? *Harvard Business Review* 86(12): 78–86.

Simon, H. (1969). *The "Sciences of the Artificial"*, Cambridge, NY: MIT Press, p. 55.

Verganti, R. (2006). Innovating Through Design. *Harvard Business Review* 84(12): 114–122.

Verganti, R. (2009). *Design-Driven Innovation: Changing the Rules of Competition by Radically Innovation What Things Mean*, Boston: Harvard Business Press.

Verganti, R. (2010). *One Size Does Not Fit All in Innovation (and Never Will)*. Available at: http://blogs.hbr.org/cs/2010/04one_size_does_not_fit_all_in_i.html.

Vogel, C.M. (2009). Notes on the Evolution of Design Thinking: A Work in Progress. *Design Management Review* 20(2): 16–27.

Walters, H. (2009). Inside the Design Thinking Process. *Business Week*, December 14th.

Walters, H. (2011). Can Innovation Really be Reduced to a Process? *Fast Company's Co Design*. Available at: http://www.fastcodesign.com/1664511/can-innovation-really-be [Accessed September 27, 2011].

5
Behavioural Strategy

Julie Verity

A 13th-century poet Ibn Yamin Faryumadi described four types of man:

- One who knows and knows that he knows – *his horse of wisdom will reach the skies.*
- One who knows, but doesn't know that he knows – *he is fast asleep, so you should wake him.*
- One who doesn't know, but knows that he doesn't know – *his limping mule will eventually get him home.*
- One who doesn't know and doesn't know that he doesn't know – *he will be eternally lost in his hopeless oblivion*! (Wikipedia 2012).

The words were re-used and popularised afresh by Donald Rumsfeld – the then US Secretary of Defence, in a press briefing in 2002 (Defence Government Transcripts). The context was a question about the Iraq war and the existence of weapons of mass destruction:

Q: Is there any evidence to indicate that Iraq has attempted to or is willing to supply terrorists with weapons of mass destruction? Because there are reports that there is no evidence of a direct link between Baghdad and some of these terrorist organizations.

Rumsfeld: Reports that say that something hasn't happened are always interesting to me, because as we know, there are known knowns; there are things we know we know. We also know there are known unknowns; that is to say we know there are some things we do not know. But there are also unknown unknowns – the ones we don't know we don't know. And if one looks throughout the history of our country and other free countries, it is the latter category that tend to be the difficult ones.

And so people who have the omniscience that they can say with high certainty that something has not happened or is not being tried, have capabilities that are ... . Yeah. [these people] can – (chuckles) – they can do things I can't do (laughter).

So, the strategy of the US and UK governments in their offensive action against Iraq early in the millennium was founded on the 'known known' that weapons of mass destruction existed inside Iraqi borders and that Saddam Hussein was capable of deploying them. As we now know, this information was flawed and in reality the strategy was predicated on an 'unknown unknown'; US and UK governments did not know the actual state of weapon development in Iraq and appeared not be aware of their imperfect knowledge.

In his briefing to the press, Rumsfeld said that without infinite knowledge there were limits to his abilities. This is a brave and unusual admission for leaders of high rank and responsibility to make, for surely it is the reason they are at the top of the hierarchy and are making strategic decisions, because they have proven themselves to be reasoned and capable analysts. Also, he must have access to vast amounts of intelligence as well as having years of experience to draw on? Even with all this at his disposal, Rumsfeld states that his effectiveness is limited by the knowledge he doesn't have and doesn't know he doesn't have.

Over 60 years ago Herbert Simon (1947) observed that people in organisations do not always act on perfect information, or make purely rational decisions. He proposed the reason for this was the cognitive limitations of our minds. Simon used the term 'bounded rationality' to describe this. Despite this early seminal work and since then, many other excellent and persuasive studies, the popular 'text book' description of strategy remains a logical, optimising process that largely depends on 'unbounded rationality', that is:

– decisions are made on sound information
– thorough analysis reveals all the information that is relevant, and
– choices are made between the available options that maximise the chance of goal achievement for the decision-maker.

It seems that acting within the 'known, knowns' domain is highly attractive to us, even when common sense tells us this perfection is unattainable. Why is this?

Influential researchers in the field of decision-making take a fairly dim view of our inability to act rationally. They describe how we behave as flawed – rather than natural. For example, we fall into traps (Hammond et al. 1998), we are blinded (Bazerman and Chugh 2006), we have delusions and emotions (Lovallo and Kahneman 2003, Morse 2006), we are subject to bias and act on gut feel (Kahneman et al. 2011, McKinsey Quarterly 2010a). The language used to describe our behaviour reinforces the taken-for-granted superiority of rationality.

Is this helpful? Is intuition always bad? And if it is unnatural for us to think rationally all the time, will we be able to cure our behaviour in order to be good, rational strategists? If not, what can we do?

This chapter explains that because we only have so much brainpower and only so much time, we often solve difficult problems quickly rather than rationally. We adopt rules of thumb (heuristics), rely on memory and past experience, use our gut feeling and intuition as short cuts and as ways to economise on the use of our cognitive faculties. According to the rational view, this translates into bias and mistakes in our behaviour and, ultimately, poor strategic performance.

The deceit of rationality

We think we are in control

There are many examples of projects that run over budget and over time, many strategies that never deliver the profits and/or revenues that are predicted and many mergers and acquisition deals that fail to deliver on promised synergies. Despite this evidence of the poor reliability of forecasts and predictions, we persist.

Take just one example of expert forecasters. The UK's Office of Budget Responsibility [OBR] was set up in 2010 by the Chancellor of the Exchequer to provide forecasts about the economy, free from political influence. In December 2011, Robert Chote, the leader of the new body, was questioned by a Treasury Select Committee of MPs about his Office's 2.5% revised-down growth forecast for 2012 over what had been predicted just eight months earlier. Forecasts for 2011, 2012 and 2013 were also revised downward substantially, creating an 'output gap' in terms of size of the economy of £65 bn in 2015.

At the Select Committee enquiry, one MP said that the OBR's latest report was couched in so much doubt that it amounted to 'just guessing'. Another said, 'If you were so wrong in March how do we know you are right now? You are being paid to forecast the future. This is not very good is it?' Another said that many of them 'were worried about the whole illusion of technocratic expertise surrounding the OBR'. When asked if he would do better next time, Mr Chote replied: 'If our forecasts were absolutely bang on the nail now, I would be warning you and warning myself that the chances of them remaining bang on the nail as history was revised were virtually nil' (BBC News 2011).

On the one hand it is surprising that these MPs think it is possible to make forecasts of quality despite the turmoil and complexity of influences in Europe's financial and political environment at the time. On the other, it is not, since there is a large body of evidence to show that we are over optimistic (called the *optimism* bias) about our capabilities and that we tend to believe events are less random and more controllable than they really are. The future is unknowable, it does not exist today to be predicted, but we perceive that our tools and theories combined with our brain power allow us to 'know' even about what is not yet created.

Accepting uncertainty, recognizing it as inevitable and living with it goes against the grain of who we are. It is human nature to downplay risk. Since ancestral times, confidence would have conferred benefit on those displaying it: attracting allies and resources, attracting potential mates and generally aiding individual success. Gradually, this trait has been selected-for and our minds have evolved to be self-believing (Cosmides and Tooby 1997).

This is just one of the ways our behaviour naturally departs from mindfulness. If the MPs paused to consider their exchange cited above, they would have realised the wisdom of Mr Chote's words – that he was only confident about his doubt. The ministers were behaving irrationally. The optimism bias was working subconsciously and effectively in their minds.

We admire confident people

So, it is natural for us to behave as if we know more than is possible to know and as if we are more in control than is possible to be. Confidence attracts followers and this has organisational consequences.

In a recent conversation between two of the leading researchers in the field of decision-making, Kahneman and Klein agreed that leaders are selected more often for their confident risk-taking than for inherent wisdom (McKinsey Quarterly 2010b). Kahneman said: ' . . . there really is a strong expectation that leaders will be decisive and act quickly.

We deeply want to be led by people who know what they are doing and who don't have to think about it too much....'

He went on to link this with *hindsight bias*, explaining how many lucky plays are converted into post-rationalised, stories about clever, deliberate strategies created by leaders gifted with foresight. This builds people's confidence in their choice of who to follow and in the depth of that leader's knowledge. There is also evidence that leaders and 'experts', over periods of time, become disproportionately more assured of their own abilities, which is often an unjustified belief (Tetlock 2005). Coupled with the behaviours described in the previous paragraph, we have a self-supporting circle of false confidence with no get out. This is how strategies can develop based on charisma and luck, and when they happen to be successful are often justified in the telling as visionary and heroic.

Emotion is instrumental in creating this behaviour. Counterintuitively perhaps, fear is probably providing us with this shield of confidence. Our reputation is our credibility, so we take care of what others think about us, motivated by the fear of loss of status. This makes it harder to admit mistakes than place the blame elsewhere, to external causes or 'the system' for example (sometimes labelled *attribution errors* (Ross 1977)); this is more likely to occur when there is hectic activity, pressure or stress within the system (Senge 2006, Omerod 2005, Edmondson and Cannon 2005).

Therefore, we are predisposed to follow confidence and trust confident people. To admit openly that we doubt our actions or listen actively to others who have a different point of view is subconsciously painful and unlikely to bring us organisational respect. Armed with stories of small, past successes, most likely not representative of reality, we can keep anxiety and doubt at bay and, on the positive side, we are able to take decisive action even though it is often unlikely to be rationally sound.

We are anxious when uncertain

Emotions are always part of the decision-making process (Damasio 2000, Pinker 1997). Powerful drivers of behaviour and counter to what we want to believe, they very often call the tune over reasoning and logic. Emotional responses are triggered by some of the most primitive parts of the brain and have been responsible for our survival over millennia. Fear, anger, disgust, surprise, sadness and joy, the six universally recognisable human emotions (Ekmann 1993), enable fast and mind-less reactions to external events that would have been highly beneficial in the 'on edge' dangerous world of our primitive ancestors. Because these behaviours happen with speed and without conscious thought, they are particularly hard to temper with rational reasonableness, even when their relevance is limited in our modern context (fear of snakes is commonplace but in most contemporary situations is rarely needed as a protection device).

The fear of loss, for example, makes us cautious and possessive about what we have, even when it might have little value for us (the *endowment effect*). We feel the pain of loss disproportionately more than we feel good about gains; the evidence suggests that gaining has to outweigh losses 2:1 before we are persuaded to risk making a choice for change (Kahneman 2011). Thinking about uncertainty also triggers parts of our brain to make us physically afraid (Camerer et al. 2004, Morse 2006). This gives us a predisposition in favour of the *status quo*. It also explains the *sunk cost trap* which describes our reluctance to abandon projects we have invested time, money, energy, passion and reputation in – all of which will be lost if the project is abandoned.

Loss aversion can also explain why we are often poor at making choices. Provided with a choice where the difference is small (an orange-flavoured ice cream versus a lemon-flavoured one), assuming both flavours are equally palatable, it is hard to give one up. Having both seems the best option since then one does not have to be lost.

When choices are widely different or complicated we also struggle, but probably for different reasons. In this situation, our brains appear lazy, preferring the short cut and avoiding the necessary analysis to enable taking the decision. Ariely (2009) illustrates this powerfully showing how we defer to the default option rather than have to consider a weighty choice. Again, it is easier to defer the decision to the status quo or what is already decided than to take the effort to consider a complex problem.

The human predisposition favours stability, especially when we are in a comfortable situation. Habits, routines, the expected, defaulting to the status quo are reassuring and allow our minds to expend less effort. This explains a lot about organisational life and the issues many organisations have trying to implement strategic change.

While in their comfort zones, people find it hard to risk change because of the losses they are likely to incur. Strangely, when there is uncertainty and anxiety is heightened, productivity often rises, our natural reaction being to work hard to protect against loss. But, when loss is certain and cannot be avoided, we will scramble and take many more and bigger risks in an attempt to cover-for and/or recover from our losses, often adopting a mindset of 'what else have we got to lose?' As Kahneman summarises: 'Utility [the value people place on something] cannot be divorced from emotion, and emotion is triggered by changes. A theory of choice that completely ignores feelings such as pain of losses and the regret of mistakes is…unrealistic.'

We are not islands

In one of Kahneman's web seminars (Edge 262, 2008), he gives examples of how psychologists have demonstrated our susceptibility to being primed by environmental cues. One of these describes how people are placed in front of a computer and asked to watch the screen on which appear words such as grey, frail, wrinkles, walking stick. Participants are then told that this part of the experiment is over and for the next stage they have to move to the other end of the building. The true focus of the experiment is on the effect these words have on the behaviour of the participants, which is measured by the pace at which they walk from one part of the experiment to the next. The result is that people walk measurably slower. The word old is never mentioned on the computer screen, but people change their behaviour and walk as if they are older, because they have heard words that are associated with being old.

There are many more examples of experiments which confirm our susceptibility to priming, and Kahneman concludes: 'We have a hugely powerful bias against the environment as a determinant of our behaviour . . . . . [but] It turns out that the environmental effects on behaviour are a lot stronger than most people expect.'

These experiments show how susceptible we are to what is going on in the environment around us. Our senses are receiving stimuli all the time, and these are prompting memory recall of feelings and closely associated events and thoughts, all of which influence the way we behave. Some of these behaviours have been known about for some time. Anchors, for example, are so called because they are pieces of information, given to us or that exist in the environment that our minds lock onto as points of reference.

For example, if you pose an open question like 'What is the population of Turkey?' people mostly don't know the answer and make a wild guess. The range of answers is scattered over a wide range.

Whereas, if the question contains an anchor 'Is the population of Turkey greater than 65 m?' answers fall in a tighter range clustered more strongly around the reference point of £65 m. These anchoring effects are among the most widely tested and reliable results of experimental psychology (Kahneman 2011) and are among the most important influencers in strategic decision-making.

The following case study illustrates how strategic decisions are influenced by anchors and other signals from the environment.

Case study: efficiency improvement strategy for a service delivery organisation

In 2009, a significant investment proposal was made to the board of a national company to consolidate regional operations. The plan involved building one new facility, closing and selling eight smaller, dispersed sites and relocating staff. The case was justified on a three-year payback, funded through significant efficiency improvements from the new organisation and sale of existing sites at favourable prices.

The strategy was presented at four separate review panels before it was authorised fully. The strategy team did an 'excellent' job of preparing and influencing key decision-makers before each meeting, and this 'effective' stakeholder management meant that the strategy was agreed painlessly by each panel in succession. This was the accepted cultural practice within the organisation.

Building the new facility is on schedule, but sale and closure of the small units is significantly delayed by resistance of both employees and local communities, who have organised an effective PR campaign.

Evidence existed, in 2009, that the most efficient operations across the national network of more than 700 units were those that employed less than 50 people.

The thoughts of the team reviewing progress in 2011 are represented in the graphic below, illustrating how each individual might reflect on the reasons why implementation has not been a success.

At the strategy team review, the leader reflects on how heavily he was primed by information contained in the independent review supplied at the planning stage. The recommendation for consolidation *anchored* his mind as a solution, very early in the project, something he only recognised with hindsight. Also, the assumptions used to build the cost model for the project were *anchored* by the hurdle rates set by shareholders before authority to go ahead could be won. Another person

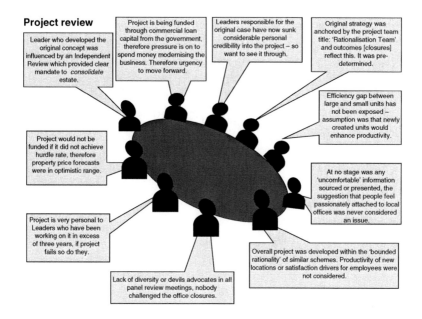

Project review

Leader who developed the original concept was influenced by an Independent Review which provided clear mandate to *consolidate* estate.

Project is being funded through commercial loan capital from the government, therefore pressure is on to spend money modernising the business. Therefore urgency to move forward.

Leaders responsible for the original case have now sunk considerable personal credibility into the project – so want to see it through.

Original strategy was anchored by the project team title: 'Rationalisation Team' and outcomes [closures] reflect this. It was pre-determined.

Efficiency gap between large and small units has not been exposed – assumption was that newly created units would enhance productivity.

Project would not be funded if it did not achieve hurdle rate, therefore property price forecasts were in optimistic range.

At no stage was any 'uncomfortable' information sourced or presented, the suggestion that people feel passionately attached to local offices was never considered an issue.

Project is very personal to Leaders who have been working on it in excess of three years, if project fails so do they.

Overall project was developed within the 'bounded rationality' of similar schemes. Productivity of new locations or satisfaction drivers for employees were not considered.

Lack of diversity or devils advocates in all panel review meetings, nobody challenged the office closures.

at the table recognises the *anchor* in the name given to the project implementers: the Rationalisation Team. At each approval stage, the team *primed* the decision-making board to concur with their recommendations. This process probably included very positive *framing* of the information being given to the board.

At the early stage of the strategy, there was an urgency to 'get on with it' and to capitalise on available funds. The environment was *priming* the team to act quickly, stimulating emotional energy and by inference *emotional* thinking. In the wider environment, 'out there' across industries, it was generally accepted that larger units equated to greater efficiency. The project process mimicked what had happened elsewhere in that similar schemes had the same loci of attention – that is, on buildings, money and hard factors rather than on the people involved. Hence, this project was anchored on previous experiences and primed by current-day signals from the environment.

Apart from anchoring and priming affecting this team's performance, there are examples of other behaviours. For example, the independent reviewers were highly credible consultants. The brand name of these created a trust in the relevance and robustness of the information that was to ground the strategy. There was an *input bias* at work here (Schweitzer and Chinander 2003). The assumption was that because the consultants' knowledge was relevant in a different context, it would translate to this situation and deliver similar quality results.

Stakeholder emotions and feelings were ignored. No time was given to consider the *losses* staff might experience, nor what the knock-on effects of these *emotions* might be. The strategy was highly focused on the physical aspects of buildings, land and money, and this strong *focus* created real and dangerous exclusions.

Sunk cost behaviours are evident not only in terms of investment in new buildings but also in personal credibility and reputation. There are many reasons to save face and resist facing the facts about the likely poor outcomes of the strategy at this late stage.

Optimism is evident in the thinking processes.

Can we cure our behaviour?

The number of our cognitive limitations and associated behaviours is long. There are many more examples of the way our behaviour results from fast, impulsive thinking that is natural to us. To date, the prescription for a cure has been 'forewarned is forearmed'. The logic is that by being aware of how we think and behave, we can instil some 'best practices' into the strategy process to correct them. Inclusions like making sure there is diversity of thinking in the team and introducing a devil's advocate to challenge assumptions. While all are worthy and sound recommendations, these solutions are about creating discipline and reigning-in our natural impulses. This requires mental energy and effort and a bit like the person who wants to loose weight, but naturally succumbs to temptation, we are likely to fail sometimes, especially when our minds are busy and/or tired with the stresses of work pressures and distractions or there is an urgency to deliver.

According to a recent paper (Kahneman, Lovallo and Sibony, 2011) team work and a 12-point check list will improve performance more than self-awareness and discipline. The underlying principle is that while it is difficult to know your own shortcomings, it is easier for others to spot yours. Designers are likely to have different anchors and frames compared with engineers. Brand managers will have different information at the top of mind compared with finance experts. Strategists could be anchored in a particular model of thinking or are using their expert knowledge, recalling from memory a similar situation and responding according to what 'worked before'. Any one of the team might see it as their pet project and not want to let it go and others will be able to read this effect and counter it. The checklist acts as a quality control mechanism on decision-making. And, as one proponent of the checklist idea said: 'Man is fallible, but maybe men are less so' (Gawande 2011).

While checklists have been shown to improve the reliability of decisions in different contexts, they don't always work for other reasons. Ticking boxes from a list does not fit with the image of being 'professional', argues Gawande (2011) who writes about doctors diagnosing and performing life-saving procedures:

> We have the means to make some of the most complex and dangerous work we do...be more effective than we ever thought possible. But the prospect pushes against the traditional culture of medicine, with its central belief that in situations of high risk and complexity what you want is a kind of expert audacity.... Checklists and standard operating procedures feel like exactly the opposite, and that rankles many people.

The appeal of 'expert audacity' is not restricted to clinicians. As we argued earlier, confidence and the ability to be in control stimulates respect and wins status and reputation for the hero. Klein (McKinsey Quarterly 2010b) called this the John Wayne style of leadership – the man who 'sizes up the situation and says, "Here's what I'm going to do"' is persistently attractive.

Are heuristics always bad?

It is hard to correct our natural behaviour with formal strictures. While these might be good medicine, we are naturally bad at taking the cure. The next step then is to challenge that natural always equals bad. Maybe there is value in doing what comes naturally, rather than trying to discipline ourselves to be something we are always going to struggle with? In the distant past the capability to see and respond quickly helped us survive in an unpredictable and dangerous world. Today's business world is littered with uncertainty and complexity. Is there a case for exploring how our ability to think fast with limited information might be advantageous?

Of interest here is the work of Klein (1998), who was fascinated by the way some experts could make fast and smart decisions with *less* information. He observed how firefighters, working under extreme pressure, having to make life-and-death decisions in minutes, developed their decision-making expertise. He discovered that they had a thinking process:

(1) they set an aspiration about what could be done in this situation,
(2) followed by selecting a course of action, and
(3) tested this out in their minds against pre-learnt repertoires
(4) stopping, if this course met the aspiration and
(5) implemented.

If the first course of action does not meet the pre-set aspiration, then another solution is tested. It works like a decision tree, where branches of yes/no answers to simple questions arrive at stop-and-act decisions if the goal can be achieved, or go on to the next line of thinking if the goal is not achieved. Time is the scarce resource and the solution is to move into action as quickly as possible by knowing which cues from the environment match with the behavioural response most likely to reach the goal.

Grand master chess players appear to use the same process of thinking, drawing on their memories of many hours of play to test-out possible winning strategies very quickly. Their ability is grounded in ignoring many possible plays and focusing on just a few important indicators in the terrain that their memories tell them are the most critical.

An example is US flight 1549 which, after take-off from LaGuardia Airport, NY in 2009, encountered engine problems. There were 155 passengers and crew on-board and the pilot, Captain Sullenberger, returned them safely after making what had to be a quick decision to land the plane on the Hudson River. Captain Sullenberger had been flying jets for 40 years. It was highly unlikely that he had time to rationally assess his options and make the calculus that would allow him to judge the best decision. But, this intuitive decision, in a highly complex and uncertain situation, resulted in a safe landing and no deaths.

So, there are circumstances when simple decision strategies, based on sets of rules that use *less* information to make fast decisions, are superior. Appropriately, Girgerenzer and Todd (1999) label these 'fast and frugal heuristics'. In this case, simple heuristics are not *irrational*, they actually make us more successful.

The problem for strategists is recognising when they can trust their expert intuition. Chess, firefighting, landing passenger jets, games of poker and warfare are all examples of environments where robust and accurate patterns form which can be recognised by practitioners over the longer term. And hence, with practice, they can 'read' the critical cues and learn to ignore the noise. But, contexts like the stock market (future share price valuations) and political events are too complex and uncertain to support formation of reliable patterns (Kahneman and Klein 2009). Therefore, while it is appealing to think we can strategise with our learnt intuition, the environment is the determinant of whether we can acquire this capability or not, and it is dangerous to assume that expertise will transfer from one context to another.

This is a relatively new field of enquiry and one that is likely to bring new and more useful insights into the future. But, Girgerenzer (2005) finds a positive argument for thinking more richly about heuristics than that taken by the 'bias and mistakes' school. He argues that heuristics are the superior way for a mind to make decisions when the world is uncertain and there is simply too much information for our brains to compute. If we did absorb and analyse all there was to see, hear and feel, we would be paralysed by data. Instead, the brain filters information, classifies and categorises it and selects the cues that are meaningful and then takes an informed bet. Sometimes, the bet is wrong and errors occur. But, getting it wrong is the road to learning and improvement. Without the failure, there is no learning and the animal cannot become more intelligent. Hence, there are 'good errors' which rational strictures would only constrain and make us less able to learn.

What can be done?

Design

The way we make decisions is complex and prescriptions are hard to find that satisfy the many facets of our wonderful minds. But, a deeper understanding about how we behave is bringing new ideas to practice. One is to design interventions that promote challenge *and* are naturally appealing.

The pre-mortem is one idea that meets these criteria. Rather than hold a post-mortem to capture learning after the event, the idea is to challenge the team to think forward before adopting a new strategy to find fault lines and possible weak spots. This can be set up as a competition or a storytelling exercise (Klein 2007). He explains (McKinsey Quarterly 2010b):

> The logic is that instead of showing people that you are smart because you can come up with a good plan, you show you're smart by thinking of insightful reasons why this project might go south. If you make it part of your corporate culture, then you create an interesting competition: 'I want to come up with some possible problem that other people haven't even thought of'. The whole dynamic changes from trying to avoid anything that might disrupt harmony to trying to surface potential problems.

As Klein describes, the pre-mortem process is designed to accommodate how people in groups naturally behave. Groups mostly display cooperative behaviour. Hence our fundamental dislike of open criticism with close clan members. Also, once a strategy is formulated and has won commitment by all the team, there is a sunk cost element which deters the voice of the devil's advocate being heard. *Herd* behaviour is also common in groups. This heuristic is useful, but dangerous in that members of the group are happy to follow the informed decision-makers who have done the complex thinking, abrogating their responsibility to think it through for themselves. The pre-mortem appeals because it challenges individuals to think and write down their own ideas without directly picking-apart those that are owned by others in the team.

Deconstruct

We need more ways to build automatic and natural behaviour into strategy processes. An analogy is how traffic calming has proved more successful by putting constraints into the actual fabric of the infrastructure. Like road bumps and road-narrowing schemes. These have proved far more successful than signs commanding motorists stick to a speed limit. Another example is in practice in Italy, where instead of accumulating points on offenders' driving licences for exceeding the speed limit, every driver starts with 12 points and has them subtracted with each offence. The sense of loss is more painful than is the feeling about gaining equivalent points, and it modifies driving behaviour more effectively. We are still learning about how to build these processes, but other chapters in this book provide leading-edge ideas. Many of these revolve around deconstructing some of the more traditional strategy behaviours. From a behavioural perspective, we know that teams perform better when there is less formality in the work setting, minimal hierarchy between members and maximum sharing of rich sources of information (Moscovici and Doise 1994). This is also how we work best naturally. Releasing strategy from the seriousness of the 'board room', from its formal presentation in papers and weighty documents, simply reducing the importance of strategy itself could make strategy more democratic, more integrated into the life of the organisation, and could reduce issues of inertia, lack of challenge and frequency of bias and 'bad errors'.

Discover

We know that confidence and certainty are appealing, but that they are dangerous. Globalisation is increasing the complexity of our working environment. Organisations are looking outside for collaborators and growth opportunities. Leaders need to resist the comfort of the known known domain. This will come from managing the level of curiosity and failure in the organisation which, in the right size pieces, will be beneficial. Doubt keeps us alert and prevents against complacence. Good errors promote learning. Strategic processes that are full of questions and challenge, ones that keep choices open for as long as possible for further exploration and by more people with different ideas, are likely to be more successful than those relying on the man who knows and knows that he knows. When Klein was asked what type of leader he would celebrate if the John Wayne style could be replaced with something wiser, he replied:

> I met a lieutenant general in Iraq who told me a marvellous story about his first year there. He kept learning things he didn't know. He did that by continuously challenging his assumptions when he realised he was wrong. At the end of the year, he had a completely different view of how to do things, and he didn't lose credibility.

By inference, this lieutenant understands the benefit of making 'good errors'. He was open to his mistakes, and presumably changed his actions to align with the things he learnt from his new environment and the people around him.

To prevent cognitive ease, strategists need to 'get out more' and, *not to places they normally go*. Literally stepping outside of the clan, using external reference points, seeing and more importantly feeling the problem and the solution from the customers' or competitors' point of view and generally being contrary will act as critical evidence sources. This will help reduce the feeling of control and very high confidence levels that are so dangerous in strategy making. Skill will then be required to bring dissenting information back to the clan to be incorporated into the strategy.

Define purpose

Finally, people are poor at making choices and are easily swayed towards the slightly sweeter-flavoured lemon ice. Having guiding principles for the organisation, knowing what the purpose of the enterprise is can be a strong defence to poor decision-making. This could be one place where the solid ground of 'knowing' is vital to sound strategy.

References

Ariely, D. (2009). *Ted Talks.* Available at: http://www.ted.com/talks/dan_ariely_asks_are_we_in_control_of_our_own_decisions.html.

Barkow, J.H., Cosmides, L. and Tooby, J. (1993). *The Adapted Mind – Evolutionary Psychology and the Generation of Culture,* Oxford: Oxford University Press.

Bazerman, M.H. and Chugh, D. (2006). Decisions without Blinders. *Harvard Business Review* 84(1): 88–97.

BBC News (2011). *Robert Chote Defends OBR Economic Growth Forecasts.* Available at: http://www.bbc.co.uk/news/uk-politics-16048137?print=true.

Camerer C.F., Loewenstein G. and Rabin M. (eds). (2004). *Advances in Behavioural Economics,* Pittsberg: Princeton University Press.

Cosmides, L. and Tooby, J. (1997). *Evolutionary Psychology: A Primer.* Centre for EP at ECSB website. Available at: http://www.psych.ucsb.edu/research/cep/primer.html.

Damasio, A.R. (2000). *The Feeling of What Happens: Body, Emotion and the Making of Consciousness,* London: Vintage.

de Gues, A. (1997). *The Living Company, Growth, Learning and Longevity in Business,* London: Nicholas Brealey.

Defense Government Transcripts (2002). Available at: http://www.defense.gov/transcripts/transcript.aspx?transcriptid=2636.

Edmondson, A. and Cannon, M.D. (2005). The Hard Work of Failure Analysis. *HBS Working Knowledge.* Available at: http://hbswk.hbs.edu/tools/print_iten.jhtml?id=4959&t=bizhistory.

Ekmann, P. (1993). Facial Expression and Emotion. *American Psychologist* 48: 384–392.

Gawande, A. (2011). *The Checklist Manifesto – How to Get Things Right*, London: Proflie Books.

Girgerenzer, G. (2005). I Think, Therefore I Err. *Social Research* 2(1), Spring: 195–218.

Girgerenzer, G. and Todd, P.M. (1999). *Simple Heuristics that Make Us Smart*, New York: Oxford University Press.

Hammond, J.S., Keeney, R.L., and Raiffa, H. (1998). The Hidden Traps in Decision Making. *Harvard Business Review* 76(5): 47–58.

Kahneman, D. (2008). Two Big Things Happening in Psychology Today. *Edge 262*. Available at: http://www.edge.org/documents/archive/edge262.html.

Kahneman, D. and Klein, G. (2009). Conditions for Intuitive Expertise – A Failure to Disagree. *American Psychologist* 64(6): 515–526.

Kahneman, D. (2011). *Thinking, Fast and Slow*, London: Allen Lane.

Kahneman, D., Lovallo, D. and Sibony, O. (2011). Before You Make That Big Decision. *Harvard Business Review* 89(6): 50–60.

Kahneman, D. et al. (2011). *The Marvels and Flaws of Intuitive Thinking Edge Master Class of 2011*. Available at: http://edge.org/conversation.php?cid-the-marvels-and-flaws-of-intuitive-thinking.

Klein, G.A. (1998). *Sources of Power: How People Make Decisions*, Cambridge, MA: MIT Press.

Klein, G.A. (2007). Performing a Project Premortem. *Harvard Business Review* 85(9): 18–19.

Lovallo, D. and Kahneman, D. (2003). Delusions of Success – How Optimism Undermines Executives Decisions. *Harvard Business Review* 81(7): 56–63.

McKinsey Quarterly (2010a). *The Case for Behavioural Strategy.* Available at: https://www.mckinseyquarterly.com/The_case_for_behavioral_strategy_2551.

McKinsey Quarterly (2010b). *Strategic Decisions: When Can You Trust Your Gut.* Available at: https://www.mckinseyquarterly.com/Strategic_decisions_When_can_you_trust_your_gut_2557.

Moscovici, S. and Doise, S. (1994). *Conflict and Consensus*, London: Sage.

Morse, G. (2006). Decisions and Desire. *Harvard Business Review* 61(1): 42–51.

Nicholoson, N. (2000). *Managing the Human Animal*, New York: Crown and London: Texere.

Omerod, P. (2005). *Why Most Things Fail – Evolution, Extinction and Economics*, London: Faber and Faber.

Pinker, S. (1997). *How the Mind Works*, London: Penguin Books.

Ross, L. (1977). The Intuitive Psychologist and his Shortcomings: Distortions in the Attribution Process, in L. Berkowitz (ed), *Advances in Experimental Social Psychology*, Vol. 10, New York: Academic Press.

Schweitzer, M. and Chinander, K.R. (2003). The Input Bias: The Misuse of Input Information in Judgments of Outcomes. *Organisational Behaviour and Human Decision Processes*, July.

Senge, P. (2006). *The Fifth Discipline* 2nd ed., New York: Currency Doubleday.

Simon, H.A. (1947). *Administrative Behaviour*, New York: Macmillan.

Tetlock, P.E. (2005). *Expert Political Judgement: How Good is It? How can we know?* Princeton, NJ: Princeton University Press.

Tversky, A. and Kahneman, D. (1974). Judgement under Uncertainty: Heuristics and Biases. *Science* 185: 1124–1131.

Wikipedia (2012). *There are Known Knowns*. Available at: http://en.wikipedia.org/wiki/Known_known [Accessed February 27, 2012].

6
Strategy and Human Nature

Julie Verity

This chapter explores extraordinary companies which are, counter-intuitively perhaps, places where people are encouraged to act and be natural. The idea is simple and pragmatic: if organisations are designed to align with our natural psychology, they will be more effective, efficient and successful. In other words, competitive advantage, the holy grail of strategy, can result from organising and behaving with the grain of human nature.

For an understanding of human nature, the chapter draws heavily on the work of the evolutionary psychologists and, to a lesser extent, behavioural economists. From this body of research, an understanding of our essential nature emerges with a realisation that our psychologies predispose us to certain group behaviours. The founder of Gore (Bill Gore), a US manufacturing company, and Ricardo Semler (son of the founder of Semco, a Brazilian conglomerate) observed these behaviours as being the way people worked best together and designed their organisations to accommodate these human universals. These companies are used in the chapter as case examples of how natural organisations can be created, sustained and grown, and be highly successful.

Two old axioms are at the heart of this chapter. One is reinforced – *people are our greatest asset*. The other – *structure follows strategy* (Chandler 1962) – is challenged.

Human nature and communities

The theory

Evolutionary psychologists (EPers) start from the premise that our brains are evolved like any other part of our body and, therefore, individuals are born sharing the same brain architecture as every other human being. The brain is no different in this respect from the common human architecture of the heart, the liver, our kidneys and so on. So, biologically, genetically, we are very similar.

A second premise is that at birth, the brain is not a blank slate. We have innate psychological mechanisms, often referred to as hard wiring and these are what determine our common behaviours. For example, we are born with an innate ability to learn a language. The language we learn depends on the culture we are born into and the experiences we have during our formative years. But, our brains have language-learning capability hardwired in (Pinker 1997). Culture is also a human universal. All human groups form cultures.

The third premise is that evolution is a slow process. The structure and function of our brains and bodies have been evolving for millions of years in response to the environmental pressures that existed over this period. Somewhere between one and two hundred thousand years late in this period, our species lived a wandering lifestyle in clans on the Savannah plain. Living in settled communities started with the practice of agriculture only about 10,000 years ago. This wandering, small clan, hunting and foraging way of life dominated the evolutionary period for our species, and it was in this environment that our brains and bodies evolved.

Over the last few hundred years, the very recent part of our history, life for our species has changed out of all proportion. But, many human instincts remain from the days of our Stone Age forebears, hardwired into the architecture of our brains, and it is these that dictate our universally shared psychological responses to the environment. These are described below.

The human universals – small is beautiful

We are essentially social beings. We are predisposed to make social contracts with others and live in relative proximity because this aided survival in the past. As with any contract, stacked against the benefits there are costs, which require compromises:

- the larger the clan, the greater the chance of survival against enemies, but the greater the need to find adequate resources
- group living can increase individual risks, like bullying from other clan members and the emotional stresses created in relationships
- having resources necessitates finding ways to share and allocate.

During our ancestral roaming days, human beings naturally formed fission-fusion, social networks (Dunbar et al. 2005). Fission-fusion describes a lifestyle where a large community of individuals live in dispersed camps of between 100 and 200 people, spread over a wide territory. Individuals might wander between camps and be recognised as one of the clan, in which case they will be welcomed and accommodated. Strangers would have been rare and treated with caution.

The wider network might collect together for ceremonies on rare occasions, but essentially, camps were communities where individuals knew each other and shared history in terms of relationships – social and family. This ability to 'know' other individuals who are not immediately in your physical living space is unique (among animals) to human beings and our ape cousins.

Knowledge about the community – who is related to who, who knows who, who likes who, what she says about him and who is good at what – is vital information to successful group living. In fact, one of Dunbar's (1996) studies showed that around 70% of all conversation is devoted to personal experiences and social relations (information about the clan), squeezing all of the remainder of human discourse about tasks, ideas, entertainment and the rest into 30%.

This relationship information is 'kept' in the neocortical regions (especially the frontal lobes) of our brains. Fascinatingly, Dunbar (1993) showed that the size of these areas directly correlates with the number of relationships we can naturally have and that this number is close to 150. While we can 'know' up to around 1500 other individuals (the size of a tribe in ancient times), beyond 150 the depth of the relationship diminishes considerably. So, 150 appears to be the limit for the number of people we can know and with whom we have a relationship based on trust and obligation.

The capability to form fission-fusion groups probably enabled trade activity between camps, and there are some theories to suggest that this very early and natural ability to trade successfully and cooperatively was instrumental in our phenomenal success as a species.

The human universals – fairness

A predisposition to cooperate is based on our trusting natures. But, we are only likely to trust the (average) 150 people that we know well enough to be confident that they will not renege on repaying our cooperative gestures in the future. Reciprocity is the 'deal' by which we naturally live. The notion that *if I scratch your back, you will scratch mine* is fundamental to the way we naturally want to behave. But, the risk of free-riders entering the clan increases if the group grows in size, since it becomes impossible for our brains to store the depth of information needed to track more than 150 individuals. Distance also compounds the problem of knowing the behaviours, trustworthy or not, of others because it is hard to observe them. Also, we must have mechanisms that allow us to spot those who are likely to cheat on a contract and be untrustworthy, otherwise self-interest could flourish over the possibility of mutual gain.

This explains why we are astute mind-readers and close observers of the body language of our fellow clan members. We are searching for visual cues of trustworthiness. We must also have a means to retaliate if someone cheats on us. The strategy we employ for this is one of tit-for-tat. In Ridley's (1996) words: 'What accounts for Tit-for-tat's robust success is its combination of being nice, retaliatory, forgiving and clear.'

The rules of tit-for-tat are as follows: when we meet another individual, we approach them as if they will cooperate, that is we start out being *nice*. If, however, this niceness is not reciprocated, we will punish – *retaliation*. Mostly this results in better behaviour and the reciprocation is then an act of *forgiving*. 'Niceness' prevents the players from getting into unnecessary trouble. Retaliation discourages the other side from persisting whenever defection is tried. Forgiveness helps restore mutual cooperation. Driving this behaviour is a strong, universal, innate notion of fairness. If we feel that we have been badly treated, we will want to take revenge at some time in the future. This is why tit-for-tat is the winning strategy in long-term relationships between two people. The existence of a past (we can remember unfairness and who inflicted this on us) and a future (the cheater fears retaliation in the future) implies that it makes sense to behave cooperatively in the long run, even when it might not appear to be the best short-term strategy for either person.

The human universals – status and hierarchy

Counter to how many of our contemporary groups are organised, that is hierarchically, in the Stone Age, individuals living in clans shared an ideology of egalitarianism. This is probably because hierarchy and status can only be acquired when there are excess resources and when these can be allocated asymmetrically. In the hunting and foraging bands of our ancestors, it would have been rare for resources to be in surplus or that they could be stored and hoarded. So, with little potential to accumulate excess, clans remained relatively free from hierarchy (Barkow 1992).

Most anthropologists also agree that while the sort of food men and women found was different, the work of finding it was divided between them and that the contribution made by each to the survival of the group was roughly equal. So the status of men and women was also roughly equal. Also, there were no formal institutions, no bosses or subordinates (except perhaps in terms of age), no policing mechanism or social welfare; adults were more or less at the same level.

Leadership was most likely situational. So that the best hunter would lead the hunting party, the best comic would lead the camp-fire entertainment, the best scout would lead the tracking party, the woman with the best locational memory would lead the foraging group. Leadership was fluid and based on merit and talent according to the task at hand. This was because followers would choose to follow the person they recognised as being the most likely to be successful. Leadership was conferred by followers (van Vugt and Ahuja 2010).

Throughout modern life, however, hierarchy and social stratification are everywhere. The reasoning made for this is that the traits which allow social stratification to develop would have been beneficial:

(i) *Seeking social standing*: Human beings are much concerned with their relative standing and seek to improve it. In evolutionary terms, higher status would have won the individual more mate choices and therefore greater chance of reproductive success.
(ii) *Nepotism*: Human beings tend to favour their own offspring and close relatives over others. This is natural (Hamilton 1964). Despite the fact that western cultures typically consider nepotism to be 'wrong', other cultures perceive nepotism as commonsensical.
(iii) *Social exchange and the ability to form coalitions*: One of the fundamentals of group living is the ability for social exchange and cooperation to gain mutual advantage. Playing politics is often a better strategy for survival than engaging in physical combat.

Even though hierarchy is common today, it would not have been the natural form of organisation during the long period of human evolution, and therefore we are naturally more inclined towards fluid leadership, fairness and working in reciprocal relationships.

Human nature at work

As we have seen, being in a group and collaborating are fundamental human dispositions. Having empathy for others, especially when we live near them, is a natural reaction. Harmony is won through practising reciprocal altruism, being nice and often giving gifts. The 'gift-giving' quality of many social gestures and indeed gift-giving itself deepens reciprocity and stirs positive emotions and feelings of warmth in the relationship. A gift can take on meaning about the relationship and as a result is treasured, often hoarded long after any usefulness has been exhausted.

Our intrinsic motivation to give and cooperate, however, can be crowded out or changed by money. The famous example is the observation made of parents collecting their children from nursery. In this example, the nursery manager decided to institute a fine for each minute that parents turned up late to collect their children at the end of the day. This was designed to discourage lateness, but the introduction of the fine had the reverse effect and parents' lateness increased. It seems that the fine eliminated the moral obligation parents felt to honour the nursery's closing hours. Imposing a payment effectively robs the contract of its gift-giving quality and replaces it with a simple monetary cost which some parents decided was worth incurring. The nursery is now stuck with the fine, and lateness, because reversing the contract is not possible – parents like the option and the transaction has changed fundamentally. There is no going back. Once a social obligation is changed to a financial transaction, it is broken.

In the work situation, many experiments have shown that when 'workers' are offered a very low rate of pay, a moderately high rate or nothing at all, those asked to work for free work just as hard, maybe even harder than those paid a reasonably high amount. The lowest paid perform the least well. For these lowest paid workers, it appears that the reward is so low as to make it simply not worth it. Volunteering is, it appears, a very different activity from working. Material rewards are often not the best way to promote hard work and commitment to the cause. Looking other human beings in the eye, shaking their hand, simply asking someone to do something for the shared reward of working in partnership towards a common goal are human innate motivators that mostly prove more powerful than money (Ariely 2008, Gneezy and Rustichini 2004).

Hand-in-hand with this is the understanding that when people are paid less and have low positions in the hierarchy, the result is poor self-esteem. Studies consistently show that such people suffer more often from physical and mental health problems which are not proportionate or related to poor diet or lack of other resources (Nicholson 1998). Organisations, therefore, with elaborate, bottom-heavy hierarchies populated with people who are poorly paid are likely to be poor performers in terms of productivity and ultimately profitability.

The reasoning, therefore, that the lowest paid are happy with their low status because they have less responsibility and are less stressed compared with those above them in the hierarchy is a myth. It is also a myth that disproportionately high bonuses motivate individuals to perform harder or better. Individuals are driven towards higher remuneration because they compare their status with others around about – especially their nearest comparators – and strive to match the status of those they perceive to be in closest competition. In fact, large bonuses often dazzle those who know they can achieve one. The focus of these people shifts from the work in hand to the lure and anticipation of the bonus, actually distracting them from performing well (Ariely 2008).

As human beings we make a distinction between status and prestige. Status is associated with rank gained through having more political power, control of resources or legitimate authority. Prestige is different. It is a particular type of status, one that is gained by an individual with a specialised skill and as a result receives deference and entitlements. Prestige is valued and sought by both males and females equally. This is not the case for status which is more strongly pursued by men. In the work context, this means that men are more likely to design competitive and hierarchical systems that meet their status-striving needs. Women are likely to feel less naturally 'at home' in these structures and with the behaviours that they encourage (Colarelli and Dettmann 2003).

Human organisations

It is wrong to picture the life of our ancestors as without conflict and strife, indeed Nicholson (1998) cautioned strongly against thinking that we existed as *noble savages inhabiting a harmonious Eden*. No form of organisational living and working together is likely to overcome all the costs of collaboration and the chance events of the environment. But, the evidence from a burgeoning volume of work in the area of human behaviour, neurology and different fields of psychology suggests that we have instinctive motivations to collaborate and natural ways to work together that can promote greater harmony, self-regulation and therefore efficiency and effectiveness.

So, from the theory described already, we can summarise that natural organisations are:

- small communities where people know each other and so can be tolerant and understanding of diverse personalities and where there are strong feedback mechanisms (probably through informal gossip)
- small means people can build reciprocal relationships based on being nice, retaliatory, forgiving and clear...
- ...especially when the organisation is focused on the long term, where history is likely to remain in the corporate memory and used to inform future actions
- status distinctions are minimal and prestige is favoured
- leadership is situational and based on individuals' skills and capabilities...
- ...followers select the leaders they will commit to
- roles are flexible and individuals can coalesce around and be involved with projects as they arise, meaning that few people need be excluded (and therefore potential saboteurs can also be minimised)...
- ...promoting lateral working and movement across the organisation, preventing local, isolated interest groups from forming
- transparent rules and clear procedural justice to ensure feelings of fairness pervade the organisation's internal operations and decisions
- simple but powerful reasons to exist as a group and continue to collaborate.

Can we find examples of companies that organise like this and if so are they successful, and what does this tell us about strategy? It is time to revisit Gore and some other natural companies.

i) Gore   –   *'Let's have fun and make money.'* **Gore slogan**
          'Let's make nothing but money.'   **Bear Sterns slogan.**

W.L. Gore & Associates, Inc. was founded in 1958 in the USA. As well as its famous Gore-Tex fabric, it also makes fibres and cables for electrical applications; medical products include heart patches and synthetic blood vessels; among its filtration range are assemblies for fuel cells that convert hydrogen to electricity and membranes for reducing air pollution in air-conditioning units. It makes guitar strings, ride-on cables for cyclists and performs geometrical imaging surveys for the oil and gas industry. It is hugely diverse in terms of the customer industries it serves and the products it produces, but all of these are made from one compound ePTFE – expanded polytetrafluoroethylene.

Gore is a privately owned company. It has annual revenues in the region of US$3 bn, employs 9500 people (called associates) in 30 countries worldwide. The company is among the very few to appear in every one of the US 100 Best Companies to Work For lists, a ranking that was started in 1984. It has also won positions in similar local rankings in the UK, Germany, France, Sweden and Italy.

Bill Gore set up the company 54 years ago with the aim of making money and having fun. Inspired by a book written by Douglas McGregor: *The Human Side of Enterprise* (1960) and his own observations from working experience, he was convinced that a company would work better without the stifling bureaucracy he had experienced in his 17 years at DuPont. He believed, as did McGregor, that people were not lazy, disinterested and only motivated by money, but that they were self-motivated problem-solvers who searched for and found meaning in their work. He believed that even large companies could have that small entrepreneurial feel that fostered individual responsibility and delivered creativity. He believed people would do a good job if they were given a good job to do.

Gore's basic guiding principles are as follows (www.gore.com/en_gb/aboutus/culture/index.html):

1. fairness to each other and everyone with whom we come in contact
2. freedom to encourage, help and allow other associates to grow in knowledge, skill and scope of responsibility
3. the ability to make one's own commitments and keep them

4. consultation with other associates before undertaking actions that could impact the reputation of the company.

Bill Gore's belief in human nature led him to create an organisation with human characteristics:

- Gore's facilities and workplaces are small: 'He studied at what point you get a diminishing return when a team gets too big and you don't see the synergies and the quality starts to fall. He found that when you get more than 150–200 people, it really starts to change and you get a different dynamic because people don't know each other's names' (Terri Kelly, CE, Director Magazine 2010).

This means that around Delaware, the Company's US base, there are upwards of 18 facilities within a 30-mile radius. This is not a high-profile, Google-like-plex/campus. According to one observer: 'it consists of . . . bland, low-rise buildings . . . you can drive past and think you are passing farmland . . . ' (Fast Company 2007).

Terri Kelly said: 'You might look at it on paper and think it looks costly, but you get a very different level of energy and focus because when folks feel they are just one of many they don't have the same attention or focus' (Director Magazine 2010).

- Gore takes the long-term view: 'Gore has immense patience about the time it takes to get it right and get it to market' (Bob Doak, Dundee, Scotland) (Fast Company 2007).
- 'We have a continuing commitment to our legacy of taking a long-term view, and we seek to make decisions that are consistent with this principle' (www.gore.com/en_gb/aboutus/culture/index.html).

Far away from the short-term strictures of Wall Street, the company can move at its own pace. Associates are encouraged to persist with a project and give it time to gestate. Pet projects are positively encouraged through 'dabble time' – company time given to associates for their own use. The famous story is about Dave Myers, who pursued his idea of longer lasting and better sounding guitar strings, strangely, emanating from his original dabble-time project of endeavouring to smoothen the gear-shift on his mountain bike. After working with the help of others for three years, the team finally took their idea to the Company with a proposal to go to market. The team built its own momentum over this time. Sometimes Dave asked others for help where he lacked knowledge and others offered to help when they thought they could make a contribution – and all in dabble time. The happy outcome was Elixir guitar strings, which, in 2007, outsold their closest US competitor by two-to-one (Hamel 2007).

- Reciprocity and gift-giving: 'a process of giving away ownership of the idea to people who want to contribute. The project won't go any-where if you don't let people run with it' (Terri Kelly (Fast Company 1997)).
- And, from the four basic guiding principles: 'freedom to encour-age, help and allow other associates to grow in knowledge, skill and scope of responsibility.'

Hamel (2007) described Gore's innovation process as a 'gift econ-omy'. People who have an idea will open it up and share with others who have relevant expertise and who want to commit their time and knowledge in exchange. It is mutual, based on trust and knowledge of associates' capabilities and what they have to bring to the project. Because the units at Gore are small, everybody has the opportunity to know what everyone else is doing and is skilled at.

- Status distinctions are minimal: 'How we work at Gore sets us apart, since Bill Gore founded the company in 1958, Gore has been a team-based, flat lattice organisation that fosters personal initiative. There are no traditional organisation charts, no chains of command or predetermined channels of communication' (www.gore.com/en_gb/aboutus/culture/index.html).

Gore operates with a lattice structure where there is very little hierar-chy and fluid leadership. This is designed to accommodate one of Bill Gore's fundamental beliefs – that there was little else more damaging to creativity and more wasteful of human effort than layers of stifling supervision and bureaucracy. There is structure at Gore, but it is dom-inated by teams and individual commitment. The website spells this out in a description of the company's culture: 'A fundamental belief in our people and their abilities continues to be the key to our success.' Living-out this belief means that Gore associates are hired into general work areas and allocated sponsors (not bosses) so that they can learn about their team, the objectives and the opportunities; they can then decide for themselves how they can best support the team using their own skills and knowledge.

People joining Gore find this culture hard to understand. The story of Diane Davidson seems typical. With 15 years under her belt as a sales executive in the clothing business, she was stymied by Gore's culture on arrival: 'When I arrived at Gore, I didn't know who did what. I wondered how anything got done here.' With a sponsor, but no boss, her sponsor had to keep reminding her that no one was going to tell her what to do. Eventually, Diane worked it out: 'Your team is your boss, because you don't want to let them down. Everyone's your boss, and no one's your boss' (Fast Company 2007).

There are few fixed titles in boxes on an organogram at Gore. People define their own roles to fit into gaps that exist within teams. They take time to settle into the organisation (one example was that it took 18 months for a new person to build credibility with their team and start making a contribution), but after building trust and cementing relationships, they can see where they might fit and can put their skills to best use – making a commitment that they will be trusted to deliver on.

- Leadership is situational, followers select who to follow: 'People want to be led by one person as opposed to another and we watch that in the organisation because they end up becoming the next leaders' (Terri Kelly, CE, Director Magazine 2010).

Dave Myer's story is a good example. He looked for followers and supporters in his endeavour to develop superior guitar strings, and followers sought him out and offered their help. As one associate said: 'If you call a meeting, and people show up, you're a leader' (Hamel 2007). Terri Kelly's promotion to the CE role is also indicative of the respect Gore plays to followers, many of whom were polled and asked who they would be willing to follow in this position. 'We weren't given a list of names – we were free to choose anyone in the company. To my surprise it was me', Terri said (Hamel 2007).

- Transparency and fairness: a guiding principle at Gore is – fairness to each other and everyone with whom we come in contact (www.gore.com/en_gb/aboutus/culture/index.html).

Associates are paid according to the contribution they make. This is judged by a committee made up of associates from the work area and by peers who are asked to make feedback. In the committee, associates are ranked against each other in terms of overall contribution and pay is made relatively. Associates are told into which quartile they fall. Seniority has no direct relationship to remuneration. Those who make the biggest contribution receive the greatest reward. Associates can grow their reputation and position within Gore if they are respected by their fellows. Terri Kelly said: 'You don't arrive at Gore as a leader. Candidates may have the competencies and the hard skills but they haven't built the followership.' And: 'I don't even try to manage the businesses. Because we are so diversified we want the divisions that are expert in different fields to have the right people to make those calls. My job is to make sure that the whole structure works as a system.'

- Simple, but powerful reasons to exist as a group and collaborate: the values Gore holds are universal; every company they operate in, people respond to the same incentives: 'Who doesn't want to be believed in? Who doesn't want to feel they can make a huge contribution? Most people want to be part of a team' (Terri Kelly (Director Magazine 2010)).

After one year at Gore, all associates are given stock options. Their website describes: 'We are committed to long-term, sustainable business growth, and believe that we are all in the same boat working toward that common goal' (www.Gore.com). And, Kelly asserts that most associates stay at Gore primarily because associates 'know they are in control of their own personal growth'.

In 2007, Gore earned US$1.58 bn in revenues and employed 6300 people. In 2010, revenues were reportedly nearly double at $3 bn and associate numbers had grown to 9500. This growth of about 50% per year, during the banking crisis and Western recession that followed, is indicative of a very successful company.

A search made on the Gore website with the keyword – Strategy – makes a handful of hits and these are mostly about the people strategies Gore practices. One reference is to product strategies. Further exploration of these reveals a highly innovative organisation that develops specialised products for groups of customers through long-term, intimate relationships. A story told by Ron – a Gore associate – focuses on working with firefighters to develop new protective clothing technology:

> 'At Gore, we place high value on building strong relationships with each other, with our customers, and with industry partners. And it pays off. 'We stand out in the industry', says Ron, 'and our voice is heard. I think it speaks for our integrity and our attitude towards our customers. We have a stable team with deep relationships with our customers. There is so much shared history and knowledge – this is rare in our industry.'

This is a natural organisation where strategy develops through product and industry experts and their collaborative links with customers who they seek to serve. This is a natural organisation where associates find leaders they wish to follow, select what projects they want to lead, chart their own route to find rewarding and meaningful work and, by creating this culture, generate profitable products which consistently replenish Gore's portfolio. This is a natural organisation where the culture and the overall system *are* central, have remained largely unchanged for 50 years and are what the Chief Executive pays the most attention to. Cultures will form in every human group, it is a human universal. At Gore, actively managing the culture to be human *is* the strategy.

ii)   Semco – *A company full of crazy people. A Group of nutters?* www.semco.com.br

Gore is not a lone case. Ricardo Semler, another pioneer of human nature, first started writing his company's success story in 1993 (Semler 1993) and then persisted, writing books and many articles over the first 20 years of his leadership of the family firm – Semco – based in Sao Paulo, Brazil. Over this period (up to 2003), he gave control of the company to the employees and watched over it as it transformed itself from one that struggled to survive the raging inflation and turbulent economic context in South America, to one making revenues of US$140 m and employing 3000 people. He said (Fisher 2006): 'If you look at Semco's numbers we've grown 27.5% a year for 14 years.' And, an investment of US$100 k 20 years ago would be worth $5.4 m today. The numbers speak for themselves, the Semler model of management – no heroic CE (no permanent CE at all), no formal planning, no HR department, no organisation chart, no headquarters, no growth targets – is a success. Competitive advantage at Semco is created by human beings in a 'democratic' organisation.

'Democratic' is Semler's label for his organisation, but it was founded on his and one of his early adviser's (Clovis da Silva Bojikian) beliefs that a humane organisation, where people took control of their own work domains, would be more motivated and make better decisions with no detriment to the bottom line. And so, everything about Semco and its style is participative. As in Gore, there are no bosses, no rules as such (there are some recommended behaviours), colleagues set and negotiate their own pay, colleagues recruit new people and make proposals about which businesses they want to be in. In 2006, Mr Bojikian (72 years old) was still working with Semco and explained: 'We wanted to demonstrate that the workplace could be a place of satisfaction, not of suffering. Work should be a pleasure, not an obligation. But this wasn't just some humanitarian thesis. We believed that people working with pleasure could be more productive' (Fisher 2006).

Unlike Gore, Semco has no mission statement and goes further than Gore in openly celebrating its lack of formal strategising. Despite this, the organisation transformed itself over the years, changing from a manufacturer of pumps and industrial mixers, serving a dominant customer to become a service provider of choice. The Semco website (www. Semco.com.br 2012) states: 'After successfully developing several businesses in the environmental consultancy area, facilities management, real estate consultancy, inventory services and mobile maintenance services, Semco Group is currently market leader in the industrial equipment area and solutions for postal and document management.'

This transformation was made by the people working in the company. Semler wrote in explanation of how this happened: 'Change is easy – but only if you are willing to give up control. People, I've found, will act in their best interests, and by extension in their organisation's best interests, if they're given complete freedom. It is only when you rein them in, when you tell them what to do and how to think, that they become inflexible, bureaucratic and stagnant. Forcing change is the surest way to frustrate change.'

Therefore, change at Semco starts with small steps and experiments. One of their early stories is typical: Semco's salespeople listened to their customers when they complained about the service they got from other suppliers. As a result, the same salespeople put a proposal together,

completely under their own initiative, to provide the service themselves and offered Semco 80% of the revenues they would generate
from the enterprise. It was agreed and, after proving their worth to their
new customers, the business expanded as the new Semco venture took
on more of their customers' maintenance work. From this small beginning, the enterprise grew until the people running it saw they might
need a partner to help manage the future growth potential. They found
a blue-chip partner and from an initial investment of $2000 each, five
years later, the business was worth $30 m. Semler wrote: 'The reason
it has been so successful is that our people came into it fresh, with no
preconceived strategies, and they were willing to experiment wildly'
(Semler 2000).

Semler's thesis is that established rules of strategic thinking, like
defining the business or industry that you serve, are constraining and
prevent flexibility, adaptability, and constrain creativity and innovation, characteristics that were vital to the success of his business. He
also rejects the notion of having to justify growth ideas with a business
plan, since there is no experience or information to base such a plan on.
Semco has grown and diversified successfully by deliberately disregard-
ing any notions of creating formal plans. Strategy at Semco emerges
from the people working there who see how they can solve problems
or take opportunities from within the relationships they have with customers, or from the potential in their expertise and products. Strategy
is organic and emergent and flourishes as a result of their culture and
natural organisation.

Gore is a company that leverages its competence in ePTFE into many
markets as far apart as medical, music and military. Semco is one of
those rather unfashionable conglomerates. Both are highly successful.
Both put faith in human beings *first* and protect their humane cultures
and structures in order to produce sustainable, profitable businesses.

Living companies

Gore and Semco don't stand alone, there are others but they are not
well reported, probably because in the past they have been labelled
as bizarre. There is, for example, Morning Star, a tomato company,
one that has grown from a one-man band in 1970 to a $700 m pa
revenue company over the past 40 years. Labelled a 'self-managing'
company, it shares most of the fundamentals attributed to natural

communities. It boasts high efficiency and low costs versus rivals as well as growth rates that outstrip industry comparators (Hamel 2011, www.morningstarco.com). Like Gore and Semco, it is privately owned or owned mostly by its associates and employees.

Mondragon, a small industrial town in northern Spain is home to the largest worker cooperative in the world. The Mondragon Group (www.modragon-corporation.com) was started in 1956 by a local priest. Fifty-five years ago it was a small engineering plant. Today the group is made up of 256 different companies, spread over 18 countries and has 85,000 workers, 70,000 of which own the corporation. It operates democrat-ically. Strategic decision-making is done by voting, on a one-member, one-vote system. There is a strong R&D track and companies in the group are known as leaders in their technology domains. As with other worker-owned companies, competitive advantage results from the wide and diverse knowledge and experience that is tapped in the decision-making process – often resulting in superior decisions. And, given that people are involved in the decisions, implementation is easier.

A worker likened how he felt about being in a cooperative to the way he felt about driving his own car as compared with a hire car: he treated his own car more carefully. He said: 'our motivation is higher, we try harder' (Day 2012).

Ownership is important. Thinking about an organisation with the metaphor of a machine in mind – the predominant paradigm of man-agement thinking over the past century – it is reasonable to conceive of a machine 'being owned' by someone else. But, change the metaphor and think of organisations as communities of living, human beings and it becomes distasteful, immoral even to think that a set of people 'own' another group of people. Living beings have their own purpose and while they naturally collaborate and trade in reciprocal agreements with others, their own lives are never totally given up to the needs, demands and goals of others, especially not strangers.

Shareholder value, therefore, is a difficult concept for a natural com-pany. To spend your working life making money for people who are not in your clan is not motivating and will not result in the best effort from people in the organisation. It is really only acceptable if there is reciprocity and respect in the contract, which is often not the case. Large salary differentials are also unnatural, especially where the differ-ences are perceived as unfair and inexplicable. These can be extremely damaging to the efficiency and effectiveness of the whole company, as those holding perceptions of unfairness will be demoralised, demotivated, care less and give less. Those voted into leadership positions at Mondragon (once every four years) receive salaries that are no more than six times that of other workers in the group. Having a mission statement or a financial target will not substitute for knowing that you have a stake in your own future.

Strategy and competitive advantage follow structure when the organisation is designed with our human psychology in mind.

References

Ariely, D. (2008). *Predictably Irrational – The Hidden Forces That Shape Our Decisions*, London: Harper Collins.

Barkow, J.H. (1992). 'Beneath New Culture is Old Psychology: Gossip and Social Stratification', in Barkhow, J.H., Cosmides, L. and Tooby, J. (eds), *The Adapted Mind*, Oxford: Oxford University Press.

Benkler, Y. (2011). The Unselfish Gene. *Harvard Business Review* 89(7/8): 77–85.

Chandler, A.D. Jr. (1962). *Strategy and Structure: Chapters in the History of the American Industrial Enterprise*, Cambridge, MA: MIT Press.

Colarelli, S.M. and Dettmann, J.R. (2003). Intuitive Evolutionary Perspectives in Marketing Practices. *Psychology and Marketing* 20(9): 837–865.

Day, P. (2012). *All Together Now*. In Business, BBC Radio 4, 15th January 2012. Available at: http://www.bbc.co.uk/iplayer/console/b0196tn9 [Accessed February 14, 2012].

Director Magazine (2010). *The Fabric of Success*. February. Available at: http://www.gore.com/MungoBlobs/381/294/director-article.pdf [Accessed March 20, 2012].

Dunbar, R.I.M. (1993). The Co-evolution of Neocortical Size, Group Size and Language in Humans. *Behavioural and Brain Sciences* 16: 681–735.

Dunbar, R.I.M. (1996). *Grooming, Gossip and the Evolution of Language*, London: Faber and Faber.

Dunbar, R.I.M., Barrett, L. and Lycett, J. (2005). *Evolutionary Psychology, a Beginners Guide*, Oxford: One-World.

Fast Company (1997). *You Have No Boss*. October/November. Available at: http://www.fastcompany,com/magazine/11/noboss.html [Accessed February 28, 2012].

Fast Company (2007). *The Fabric of Creativity*. Available at: http://www.fastcompany.com/node/51733 [Accessed February 14, 2012].

Fisher, L. (2006). Ricardo Semler Won't Take Control. *Strategy+Business* (41), Winter. Available at: http://www.strategy-business.com/article/05408.

Gneezy, U. and Rustichini, A. (2004). 'Incentives, Punishment and Behavior', in Camerer, C., et al. (eds), *Advances in Behavioural Economics*, pp. 572–589, Pittsburgh: Princeton University Press.

Hamel, G. (2007). *The Future of Management*, Boston: Harvard Business School Publishing.

Hamel, G. (2011). First, Let's Fire all the Managers. *Harvard Business Review* 89(12): 49–60.

Hamilton, W.D. (1964). The Evolution of Social Behaviour. *Journal of Theoretical Biology* 7: 1–52.

McGregor, D. (1960). *The Human Side of Enterprise*, New York: McGraw-Hill.

Nicholson, N. (1998). Seven Deadly Syndromes of Management and Organisation: The View from Evolutionary Psychology. *Managerial and Decision Economics* 19(7/8): 411–426.

Pinker, S. (1997). *How the Mind Works*, London: Penguin.

Ridley, M. (1996). The Ancients of Trade. *DEMOS* (10): 33–36.

Semler, R. (1993). *Maverick*, London: Century.

Semler, R. (2000). How We Went Digital Without a Strategy. *Harvard Business Review* 78(5): 51–58.

van Vugt, M. and Ahuja, A. (2010). *Selected: Why Some People Lead, Why Others Follow and Why It Matters*, London: Profile Books.

7
Strategy as Practice

Katie Best

Introduction

From experience, we all probably know that challenging the status quo can be a difficult and yet rewarding process. In our working lives, this is true both for individuals and organisations; questioning or upending common assumptions can cause conflict. However, good often comes from such a course of action. For example, while working at a business school in London, a key organisational objective was to design an innovative MBA programme that would make an impact in the cluttered MBA marketplace. As MBA Director, responsibility for achieving this objective fell primarily on me. So, I gathered the MBA team together and we started to list, on a whiteboard, the assumptions we each had about the ways in which MBA programmes are designed and delivered.

The following assumptions came up a number of times:

- Students physically attend lectures
- Students are taught modules which focus on one subject
- Students sit at desks
- Students are asked to analyse case studies.

Next, we upended these assumptions. We challenged if MBA programmes always had to be like this, and we built some of the more practical insights from this exercise into our new Masters programme. The product we finally launched:

- had no face-to-face lecturing; any lectures were pre-recorded as online sessions and the classroom became the place for workshops, discussion and rehearsal of ideas.

- was constituted with inter-disciplinary modules, straddling more than one core subject. We aimed for unusual combinations – economics and marketing, anyone?
- could be 'taught' outside traditional classroom spaces. We encouraged the use of any spaces in the building. Sometimes classes were run in the breakout areas, with the lecturer moving between groups.
- included an assessment that asked the students to *write* a case study.

None of these are entirely unique, but by shaking up common assumptions, we created a product that did represent something different to the competition and which, feedback told us, attracted students on this basis. In this example, and others, this technique has proved to be a great way of playing with ideas and working out how to change standard products or practices in ways which differentiate.

What if we did the same exercise with this thing we call 'strategy'? What if we changed the view, reframed our thinking or simply challenged assumptions which abound in the ways we talk and think about strategy. What new insights might we gain and would they lead to fruitful ideas about differentiating our strategic activity from the competition? Would it make us better strategic practitioners?

This chapter aims to present just such a challenge and, in doing so, to help improve strategic practice. It describes the work of a field of research called Strategy As Practice (SAP). SAP researchers are academics, but their aim is to observe what managers and leaders actually do rather than follow a popular academic line of telling practitioners what they *should* be doing. It upends the assumptions that some academics and consultants seem to have built into their prescriptions to business about the who, what, where, why and how of strategy.

So, before reading on, cover the page and note down what comes to mind when asking yourself the question: *What is strategy?*

From listening to academics and managers and reading text books and articles, these answers to this question are common:

- Strategy is talked about as if it is a unitary 'thing' that organisations have (e.g. *we have a strategy, there is a strategy, the strategy is the plan etc.*).
- 'The strategy' is created using a toolbox of models and analysis techniques.
- Leaders are responsible for authoring 'the strategy'.

- Strategy is created during designated workshops and away-days.
- Middle managers are the ones responsible for implementing strategy.

This list might concur, at least in part, with yours. But do the points above (and indeed the points from your own list) successfully summarise how organisational strategy looks and feels? On further inspection, you may feel that these points arise not from what you have directly experienced, but rather from what textbooks, consultants or your colleagues have told you. Your experience, if you really think about it, doesn't suggest that strategy is the way it is described above at all.

As if to demonstrate this, in *Management Myths: Why the Experts Keep Getting It Wrong,* Matthew Stewart (2009) shows how consultants keep reiterating fallacies about strategy created by academia and 'big business' consultancies, encouraging business people to organise around these 'classic' descriptions reflected in the bullet points discussed above (for a deeper story about the classic view, see Mintzberg et al. 1998 and Whittington 2004). Stewart argues that in this way what strategy is and how it comes about is sustained, but that as a description, it is for most organisations, a myth.

In the first half of the chapter you are about to read, the assumptions listed above are upended in order to introduce some of the main findings of SAP researchers to date. The second half of the chapter explores some of the implications that this process of upending creates for managers and business.

Strategy is not a thing that firms have, it is what people do

In popular management culture and academia, strategy is treated as a thing that organisations have. There are many examples, including in the work of Porter, of strategy being treated as a 'thing'. For example, Porter has said 'Having *a strategy* is a matter of discipline. It requires a strong focus on profitability rather than just growth, an ability to define a unique value proposition, and a willingness to make tough trade-offs in choosing what not to do' (Porter 2001, emphases added). In Samra-Fredericks' paper in which managers discuss strategy, we see the perspective carried from the textbook to organisational perspectives and practice, with one of the managers saying, for example, 'if you have a strategy (.) then anything else becomes irrelevant … but the danger of not having a … [strategy] is like a ship that doesn't have a rudder you don't know where the hell you end up' (quoted in Samra-Fredericks 2003: 141–142).

It is thus often taken-for-granted in these quotes that strategy is made and then fixed. The assumption is that 'the strategy' is created in strategy meetings, where conversations among a few are made tangible through the production of documents. These can be PowerPoint presentations to shareholders, five-year plans 'cascaded' to employees, glossy brochures, statements posted on websites and in annual reports, mission statements sent out as laminated 'table tents' to be displayed on office desks or as posters on walls.

It is, according to many strategists, including the one quoted by Samra-Fredericks, an item which every company should have in their inventory because it is a locus around which 'organisation' happens. Many metaphors are used to reflect the value of having a strategy – from it being the rudder of a ship (Samra-Fredericks 2003) to being the magnet which makes sure that the workforce – who are in this metaphor iron filings – is pointing in the same strategic direction (Collis and Rukstad 2008).

Because of its ability to draw people together and to act as a framework for decision-making and a locus for action, there might be some value in treating strategy as 'a thing': employees and the board have something around which to organise themselves and their conversations, and the outside world can – if allowed access to 'the strategy' or versions thereof – get a sense of the organisation as it wishes itself to be.

However, such a treatment is not without its problems: the treatment of strategy as a thing implies a degree of fixity which rarely exists. Also, most managers know that there is a disconnection between what is written about strategy and what happens in the organisation in practice. Therefore, the decision whether any of the spoken or written artefacts emanating from the board room actually 'are' strategy is challenged by those working in this field. These observers of the practice of strategy suggest that the verb – strategising – is a more helpful indicator of the reality rather than the noun – strategy:

> The essential insight of the practice perspective is that strategy is more than just a property of organizations; it is something that

> people do, with stuff that comes from outside as well as within orga-
> nizations, and with effects that permeate through whole societies.
>
> (Whittington 2004: 627)

Rather than treating strategy as a stable artefact, what about reimag-
ining it as a process – a shifting set of ever-changing activities that are
enacted by people inside and outside the organisation, such as workers,
managers, stakeholders, suppliers, customers and consultants? Strategy
may be 'set' by the board but, during and after the 'creating' of the
intent, the board has to share it and motivate others to participate
and deliver it. There are many points in this stream of activities where
diversion, accidental or not, from the intended course can occur. So,
the reality of strategy is one of multiple, various, ever-changing actions
and activities which are performed *in situ* and often at a distance from
the originators of the initial intent.

For example, Kornberger and Clegg studied the formulation of strategy by/for the city of Sydney. Their observations showed that many of
the key stakeholders saw the process of creating strategy in the meetings as more important than the outcome itself. The process allowed
a wide range of stakeholders including city workers and residents to
engage in the process. And what emerged from the process was not
really a written document – although, of course, there was one – rather,
it was the translation of 'a cacophony of voices into homogeneous
political will' (Kornberger and Clegg 2011: 150). Much of the strategic work of getting people to buy into the city's vision for itself had
been done before the document was generated. Thus, we can see in
this way that if we ignore the very nature of the process through which
this strategy is formed then we have missed the very point of strategy altogether. Thus, strategy is not best seen as a 'thing', but rather a
process – one which may create things but which is not just a thing
itself.

It is only by recognising strategy as an on-going process rather than
something static and objectified that we can see organisational strategy for what it most commonly is: a process influenced by individuals
everywhere associated with the business.

Therefore, the prescription to leaders and managers is to switch focus
to *strategising*. By studying 'all the meeting, the talking, the form-
filling and the number-crunching by which strategy gets formulated
and implanted' (Whittington 1996: 732), managers might gain fresh

insights into the successes and failures of organisational life. The formal strategy documents which might encourage us to see strategy as a fixed 'thing' are only one part of a much larger picture of strategic activity which occurs in the organisation. By reducing the focus on strategy and raising awareness about strategising, managers and leaders will be more effective strategists, and create more successful organisations.

Tools are both more and less than we assume them to be

There are a plethora of tools labelled as strategic thinking devices, including Porter's Five Forces, SWOT analysis, the Resource Based View's VRIN characteristics and so on. These are prized as part of the strategist's skill set, but there are downsides that are worth bringing to the fore, by upending assumptions about their value.

Firstly, while tools are offered as just that, a tool, or a lens through which to see the world, when used in practice they can be treated as 'stable analytic objects' which create unproblematic, seamless routes to objective plans (March 2006). Indeed, tools can become a crutch, limiting managerial thinking by discouraging the harder work of thinking creatively or differently. Because they are accepted as being the 'correct' and credible way of 'doing' strategic thinking, it is sometimes hard to ignore them in favour of a unique technique that might deliver superior strategic ideas. A tool can thus be helpful and dangerous in the same measure. It might help inspire or limit thinking. Whatever the outcome, using a model can furnish the thinker with protection from the repercussions of bad decision-making (it was the tool that made the mistake, not me) and reduce the individual's responsibility for some hard thinking. A great deal of research is now focused on showing the fallacies contained within common strategic tools and ways of thinking, both inside and outside the SAP domain (Whittington 2004; Rouleau 2005; Johnson et al. 2010 and Best 2012).

Interestingly, SAP researchers find that the value of a strategic tool in the hands of a practitioner is not necessarily that which the creator conceived. For example, Jarzabkowski and Kaplan (2008) identify that managers applying strategic tools use them as a social mechanism which helps shape conversations. Similarly, a tool guides thoughts, helps to justify decisions and forms a locus for collective attention (see also Kornberger and Clegg 2011). The quality and structure of the discussion proves to be where the organisational value is. Often the recognition that the information the tool requires is simply not available is *the* strategic learning.

Secondly, some tools may be disregarded simply because the person offering them up as a tool of value is not credible himself/herself (Johnson et al. 2010). Tools which are tainted by the poor reputation of their designers or promoters are unlikely to produce results that anyone is committed to act upon.

Thirdly, models encourage users to adopt fixed views. Generally, the strategist is placed on the periphery of the organisation, looking in (as with resource-based tools) or looking out (as with economic environment tools). They force categorisation and the creation of boundaries which in reality don't exist (March 2006). Viewing the organisation from the edge may blind the strategist, rendering them unable to see what is happening in the thick of the organisation (Frisch 2011).

Fourthly, this focus on formal, rational tools might block richer, free-flowing discussions and cause strategists to overlook other tools. For example, the normal table clutter – pens, paper, discarded sandwich wrappers, files and coffee cups – are often reached for to explain a participant's 'mental map' of what the organisation's future could be; another person might use a biro to point towards a PowerPoint slide, saying how they disagree with what this slide contains and overlaying it with a drawing in mid-air which describes another way of seeing things. And what about hands, smiles, body language – these are often displaying important strategic signals of emotional belief in or commitment to the discussion. The role of real things in doing strategy is ignored due to the singular focus on the prescribed model.

Finally, the emphasis on strategic tools as analytic devices can mean that tools for strategy implementation are overlooked. For example, a poka-yoke is a Japanese term for any mechanism in manufacturing or production which allows someone to do their job. Frederick Taylor, father of Scientific Management, redesigned workers' shovels to ensure that they were the most efficient shape for shovelling pig iron; McDonalds uses a huge range of poka-yokes, including special ketchup-squirters for the perfect amount of ketchup for a burger. If poka-yokes help McDonalds to meet its strategic aim of delivering identical 'right every time' burgers then they can also be seen as strategic tools. Even the air hostess's smile or the bailiff's frown may be seen as tools which help to get the company's strategy done (Hochschild 1983).

Thus, strategic tools are a very wide range of socially deployed resources. These are important in the process of strategising but can be used to greater effect when their limitations and advantages are fully known so that their full scope is recognised and capitalised upon.

Strategists are not confined to the C-suite

A popular taken-for-granted idea is that strategy creation is the exclusive domain of the senior management team, including the Chief Executive Officer (CEO), board of directors, non-executvie directors and the consultants called-in to help. Many textbook definitions of strategy make this assumption: even when a down–up, up–down movement of information is acknowledged, there is a persistent assumption that senior people do strategic activities which are different from operational ones. This is compounded by the military and planning references to stratifications of strategy and the idea that strategy is not the same as tactics (Mintzberg et al. 1998). Since strategy 'deals with the big picture and future, it is very important business . . . usually it is a top management privilege to spend time arguing [about strategy]' (Carter and Clegg 2008: 9–10). The hierarchical notion of big decisions and small implementation tactics creates a way of thinking that it might be useful to upend.

In my own work, for example, which has looked at volunteer tour guides in museums, this shows how tour guides' activities can be seen to reflect and recreate organisational strategy (Best 2012). They shape their talk, language and activities in ways which bring in disparate audiences and encourage engagement with historic buildings and artefacts. Museums receive their funding based precisely on how accessible they are, and so without having been specifically trained to contribute to organisational strategy, the tour guides nonetheless find themselves in an incredibly powerful and important position, being strategic actors who have an impact on the museum's abilities to survive and thrive.

The actions of the tour guides, therefore, can reflect *and* contribute positively to the organisation's strategy. These actors can deliver and provide evidence for the funding bodies of positive engagement with their visitors. Their strategic impact, however, often goes unrecognised and this oversight means that the organisation loses the opportunity to capture value and leverage strategic advantage.

Moreover, in the service sector, value emerges during the consumption experience and cannot always be embedded in a service product consumed in the absence of the service producer. As such, through their interaction with workers, the customers are always a co-creator of that value, along with employees and other resources supplied by the organisation (Ford and Bowen 2008). Often, those at the lowest level of the organisation have high levels of client contact (administrative assistants, sales clerks, theme park attendants, trainee accountants). Common practice at the frontline of the organisation can re-author the same strategic aims as originated and implemented higher up in the organisation, or it can diverge, often in the absence of a manager to control the process and bring it back on track. As such, leaders are far from the sole authors of organisational strategy; even the most junior members of staff translate strategy in their own work with clients and each other (Rouleau 2005).

But, this type of work is not routinely labelled – by either organisations or researchers – as strategic. 360° branding is an idea which emerged from the work of advertising agencies but which is now enthusiastically embraced by many contemporary organisations – in which every activity that occurs within the organisation is portrayed as a potential opportunity to reinforce brand values and as problematic if it delivers a message that is 'off brand'. When Disneyland workers 'punish' riders for being rude by over-tightening their seat belts or shortening their rides, the brand, and thus the strategy, is undermined. Frontline staff can deliver the strategy as something altogether different from the stated intent. Lots of companies 'know' that the brand is delivered by their frontline people, but do they invest in these activities as if they are 'strategic'?

By upending the thinking, there is so much more 'strategic' work that can be done 'out there' to gain competitive advantage. In particular, there is a need to recognise that even in those organisational activities which are, to the average eye, so routine as to become mundane, there is the opportunity to achieve excellence. The Olympic swimmer can only win by focusing on the minutiae of his performance, recasting these seemingly tiny and mundane acts into significant parts of the performance (Chambliss 1989). Similarly, the excellence of the most junior workers will likely be found in activities which are, at first glance, little more than mundane.

Strategy away-days reinforce the C-suite assumption

As discussed in the section above, those who have an office in the C-suite are routinely seen as being the people who 'do strategy'. A key part of organisational life which reaffirms this assumption is the strategy away-day in which an organisation's most senior, or most respected members, remove themselves from the day-to-day work of the organisation and indulge in some strategic thinking at a distance from the formal confines of the office. Leaders are seen to 'author strategy' through such workshops, which are widely believed to have significant organisational benefits. The perceived value from these offsite days appears at least in part to be derived from ritualised aspects. The use of a strategy consultant, the application of strategic tools and the psychological and geographical removal of senior staff from the organisation and the organisation's status quo all give weight to what is achieved to make it seem particularly special (Johnson et al. 2010).

However, the research as to whether such workshops have a direct strategic value to the organisation or not is inconclusive (see Johnson et al. 2010, introduction, for a discussion of this point). The fact alone that they offer perceived value by creating an opportunity to discuss and convene around important organisational topics may be sufficient to justify their occurrence. And yet, this very point may have negative aspects, reinforcing the (incorrect) assumption that strategic work is confined to those within the C-suite. By reiterating the idea that an organisation's 'important' people do the organisation's most important strategy work at these types of workshops further underlines the divide between mental models and practice. Studies of practice clearly show, as outlined in the previous section, that all organisational members are strategic actors. As such, it problematically and constantly relocates the organisation's attentions away from the nitty-gritty places where strategic work is also being done, such as on the organisation's frontline or in the back office.

In the sense that away-days take people away from the office to create a secondary environment, it creates a liminal space. By 'liminal space' is meant a space psychologically and geographically removed from the organisation. Through this degree of removal, proposed solutions often do not augur well with the organisation they are designed for (Collins 2004). Because these plans are created in a liminal space, it is often hard to integrate these ideas back into an organisation's every-day activities. Seidl et al. (2011) identify that even though a strategy workshop may be deemed a success, in that a plan is originated which seems like a good plan, this does not necessarily translate into subse-quent organisational activity. This is partly because strategies created at an away-day are made in an environment which is distinctly sepa-rate and the reality and context of the organisation – particularly its limitations – like structure and hierarchy – are lost by removing the conversation to a separate space. The ritualised nature of the strategy workshop means that the ritual itself can take over and the solutions arrived at can lead to unrealistic outcomes which would be difficult to employ in the organisation for which they were apparently designed.

Thus, to see a strategy meeting as being anything more than a small part of the strategy-making process is to misunderstand the very essence of strategy – which is that of a socially constructed and recon-structed process, not that of a thing with objectivity and fixity, which can be carved out at a meeting and considered to hold forevermore, or at least until the next strategy meeting.

Everyone is a strategic actor

Finally, SAP researchers challenge the idea that once 'designed' by the higher echelons of the organisation, followers fall into line and deliver. There is a tendency within this 'classic' approach to assume that followers will do this almost unthinkingly and without demon-strating any agency of their own.

In practice this is not our experience, and not what SAP researchers find from their scrutiny. For example, Balogun and Johnson (2005) explored how a change strategy originated by top management and enforced on middle managers was not implemented as top man-agement intended. As the strategy was filtered down through the organisation, middle managers undertook their own sense-making pro-cess on strategic communications, and in turn tried to give a sense of the new strategy to their teams. Part of the change strategy was a shift from a hierarchical to a decentralised organisational structure, which aimed to improve cross-department working. However, middle management felt that the new structure led to a feeling of increased competition between departments. Middle managers shaped what was told to them in a way which made sense of how the strategy might work at their level – something with which the top managers were unlikely to be familiar.

This demonstrates how there was a significant gulf between the 'strategy', as formulated by top management and how it is understood and enacted by the organisation. Managers make sense of strategy and share it with their teams, who in turn make sense of the strategy for themselves. Anyone who has ever played the childhood game of Chinese whispers knows that communication is an art which is hard to do. For the meaning to be intact at the end of the whisper chain is a rarity, but here there is the added dimension of managerial power and a need to change the message slightly in order to protect both department and position. Hence, strategy implementation is a process of sense-making and sense-giving and solving the problem of how to make it work rather than a seamless and effortless implementation of leadership intent.

Another example is given by Rouleau (2005). In this work, a retail manager of a fashion boutique was studied through a period of corporate strategic change. The manager shaped the information that she gave to individual stakeholders – from customers to journalists – differently to make it palatable to each of them. She selected the relevant features of the new strategy, bringing them together to make the right 'telling' for that particular stakeholder. For example, pointing out that it would be 'mid-market' to a journalist looking to 'place' the collection in relation to other collections, but talking to a customer about a new, softer, more feminine look, playing into her own interest about what the clothes are going to look like and whether they will suit her lifestyle. There were commercial benefits to creating stories about the strategy to suit individual stakeholders. The organisation appears to achieve a successful result in light of the boutique manager's careful engagement with the strategy. The ultimate goal of commercial success makes it rational and relevant to help different stakeholders make sense of the new organisational strategy in different ways rather than seeing the strategy in exactly the way in which it has been presented to the boutique manager herself.

The idea that strategy is thought of by a few, disseminated to unthinking, passive followers and then implemented does not hold. This forces us to think instead of the organisation as filled with people who can each influence strategic activity in potentially dramatic ways. It emphasises the need for sense-giving by those responsible for strategic direction and reminds sense-makers of their need to seek clarification if they wish to conform.

Implications of strategy as practice research for practising managers

Upending assumptions has the potential to give a new perspective and find new insights. This is a good enough reason to challenge some of the more conventional ways we think about and do strategy, simply to make sure that the process is the best it can be. So, in summary, what are the messages that this relatively young field of research has to offer the practicing manager?

See strategy as a process (not as a thing)

Too often, strategy is seen as a unitary thing, a document which is put on the shelf while the organisation gets on with things. Seeing strategy as a thing disallows it from being seen as the messy, human process that it is. This means that companies do not capitalise on opportunities to make strategising a more effective process, losing out on potential competitive advantage as a result. For example, if an organisation can identify strategy workshops as a place where their strategy often becomes derailed, they can take preventative or corrective action. Most often, the organisation's most expensive people are involved with strategic work, making it a costly activity. So understanding when the process delivers good or bad outcomes and how it works in company-specific contexts will promote the best use of resources.

Additionally, thinking about strategy as a process will enable managers to influence strategic direction more effectively. By seeing themselves as actors in a process, (a) individuals can deliberately and actively manage their own organisational influence and (b) leaders will be able to recognise, encourage or guard against such influence.

Reconsider who does organisational strategy

Currently, strategy is understood as something which top managers author and middle managers implement. However, by recognising that strategic work happens all over the organisation, the manager can seek to make the organisation's practices more strategically effective. For example, call-centre workers, tour guides and office cleaners are very rarely seen as strategic actors. However, here the perception that these roles have low strategic value is challenged, encouraging decision-makers to revisit how personnel are recruited, trained and managed. And if there are changes which need to be made to bring their work into line with the desired strategic direction, the benefits to the organisation could be significant for relatively small cost outlays.

Rethink what an organisation's strategic tools are ...

Managers may now wish to consider a wider range of organisational artefacts as strategic tools. The category of 'strategic tools' doesn't have to be limited to the handful of abstract models that the company chooses to use, but can include a much wider range of 'things', too. Strategic tools can be seen to include, but not be limited to, the organisation's buildings, equipment and workers, ranging from the board room to the shop floor, a PowerPoint presentation to a cup or a smile. Reconsidering the objects that an organisation actually uses to enact its strategy and focussing on 'things' will help organisations to create environments more conducive to successful deployment of strategy. Equipment will be bought, rooms designed and smiles deployed in ways which are conducive to, and encourage, strategic processes.

... and get the most from strategic tools

Tools are good, many are better than one and finding those that best fit with the specific organisational issue is necessary. Tools can also constrain and become habitual. Upending and challenging when to and which to use and what behaviours these tools are encouraging will promote best strategic practice.

Work hard to achieve value from away-days and workshops

Away-days increase communication flows between participants, galvanise the team which participates and create a common language. However, they do this in isolation, both psychologically and geographically. They are elitist, raise expectations and send many signals to the rest of the organisation that might be surprisingly counter to what the strategy team is trying to achieve. The challenge is not to take them for granted. Leaders should look hard at the objectives of away-days, challenge if this is the best way to achieve the objectives and ask what other styles, formats, processes might produce better outcomes.

Re-think how to develop strategists

By re-imagining the strategic life of an organisation in the way this chapter argues, there are more people who need to be trained as strategists, and all need a different approach from the 'classic' view. Leaders will need to rethink where and how to use their power to influence the strategic process and ultimately steer in the desired direction. Frontline staff will need more information about their role and how vital this is to achieving the big picture; they will need to know how the organisation joins up and how those links deliver value or destroy it. Those in the middle of the organisation's hierarchy are likely to be aware of their power to support or disrupt the strategic direction (Balogun and Johnson 2005), but recognising their importance as sense-makers and sense-givers should result in leaders spending more time sharing richer quality information with them.

Conclusion

And so we return to the strategy workshop introduced at the beginning of this chapter where we were trying to design an innovative MBA. The workshop prompted us to question common assumptions about the content of an MBA programme and to create fresh insight and approaches in doing so. The aim of this chapter was similar: to question common assumptions, to identify possible innovations and to explore approaches for benefiting from these innovations.

The MBA workshop did not result in a definitive strategic plan which was stuck to rigidly in the subsequent delivery of a new programme. Rather, the ideas started a process of activities and conversations among people in the organisation. The strategy workshop was conducted with a privileged few, separated from the normal activities of the organisation. When the resulting documentation and ideas were introduced to others in the organisation, each made their own sense of it and gave their own sense of it in the way they presented it to others – everyone from the Dean of the Business School to the telephone sales team and eventually, potential students. The workshop was successful but only in the limited sense that it started a process of interpretation and activity among other strategic actors. The workshop thus provided a useful lens through which to look at the world, but the lens does not make changes, redistribute resources, create new products and sell them – people do that. The value SAP research brings is in challenging some of the assumptions that we might hold about strategy as described by the 'classic' view. By studying the reality of strategy in practice, we are able to see the familiar as unfamiliar again.

This chapter's advantages and limitations are similar to the limitations of the workshop; it creates a liminal space – an opportunity for the manager to rethink some common assumptions about strategy and to influence future strategic practices for individual and organisational gain. In itself, however, it is not a solution to strategic problems: it can be seen as a new tool in the manager's strategic toolbox – maybe a lens through which the world becomes a little clearer, helping each subsequent strategic activity to make a little more sense than the last.

References

Balogun, J. and Johnson, G. (2005). "From Intended Strategies to Unintended Outcomes: The Impact of Change Recipient Sensemaking". *Organization Studies* 26(11): 1573–1601.

Best, K. (2012). Making Museum Tours Better: Understanding What a Guided Tour Really is and What a Tour Guide Really Does. *Museum Management and Curatorship* 27(1): 37–41.

Carter, C. and Clegg, S. (2008). *A Very Short, Fairly Interesting and Reasonably Cheap Book About Studying Strategy*, London: Sage.

Chambliss, D.F. (1989). The Mundanity of Excellence. *The Mundanity of Excellence: A Report on Stratification and Olympic Swimmers* 7(1): 70–86.

Collins, R. (2004). *Interaction Ritual Chains*, New York: Princeton University Press.

Collis, D.J. and Rukstad, M.G. (2008). Can You Say What Your Strategy Is? *Harvard Business Review* 86(4): 82–91.

Ford, R.C. and Bowen, D.E. (2008). A Service-Dominant Logic for Management Education: It's Time. *Academy of Management Learning and Education* 7(2): 224–243.

Frisch, B. (2011). Who Really Makes the Big Decisions in Your Company? *Harvard Business Review* 89(12): 104–111.

Hochschild, A. (1983). *The Managed Heart: Commercialization of Human Feeling*, Berkeley, CA: University of California Press.

Jarzabkowski, P. and Kaplan, S. (2008). Using Strategy Tools in Practice: An Exploration of 'Technologies of Rationality in Use'. *Academy of Management*, Anaheim, California.

Johnson, G., Prashantham, S., Floyd, S.W. and Bourque, N. (2010). "The Ritualization of Strategy Workshops." *Organization Studies* (October). Retrieved October 13, 2010 (http://oss.sagepub.com/cgi/doi/10.1177/0170840610376146).

Kornberger, M. and Clegg, S. (2011). Strategy as Performative Practice: The Case of Sydney 2030. *Strategic Organization* 9(2): 136–162. Retrieved March 20, 2012 (http://soq.sagepub.com/cgi/doi/10.1177/1476127011407758).

March, J.G. (2006). Rationality, Foolishness, and Adaptive Intelligence. *Strategic Management Journal* 27(3): 201–214.

Mintzberg, H., Ahlstrand, B. and Lampel, J. (1998). *Strategy Safari: The Complete Guide Through The Wilds Of Strategic Management*, London: FT Prentice Hall.

Porter, M. (2001). Strategy and the Internet. *Harvard Business Review* 79: 3.

Rouleau, L. (2005). Micro-Practices of Strategic Sensemaking and Sensegiving: How Middle Managers Interpret and Sell Change Every Day. *Journal of Management Studies* 42(7): 1413–1441.

Samra-Fredericks, D. (2003). Strategizing as Lived Experience and Strategists Everyday Efforts to Shape Strategic Direction. *Journal of Management Studies* 40(1): 141–174.

Seidl, D.N., MacLean, D. and MacIntosh, R. (2011). Rules of Suspension: A Rulesbased Explanation of Strategy Workshops in Strategy Process. in *71st Annual Meeting of the Academy of Management*. San Antonio, TX.

Whittington, R. (1996). Strategy as Practice. *Long Range Planning* 29(5): 731–735.

Whittington, R. (2004). Completing the Practice Turn in Strategy. *Organization* 27(5): 613–634.

8
Strategy and Discourse

Gill Ereaut

The enigma of organisational culture – analysing language as a practical approach

There is a significant literature on corporate culture and recognition of its influential role in organisation success (Deal and Kennedy 1982, Schein 1999, 2004, Johnson et al. 2011, Jaruzelski et al. 2011). Yet culture is also known to be difficult to pin down and make tangible, and cultural change is notoriously slow and difficult to bring about. This chapter offers a rigorous, tested and effective method for working with organisational culture, showing how, when hidden cultural assumptions are revealed, systemic change and strategic innovation become possible.

The method is grounded in discourse analysis and linguistics, analytic tools which show the hidden patterns within an organisation's language. These language patterns matter because they consistently both reflect and maintain organisational culture, but they are hard to see for those inside because language becomes invisible when it is familiar. In our experience, the intangibility but tenacity of an established culture is a particular strategic problem for large and long-established organisations trying to keep pace with shifting contexts or conditions but struggling to encourage or bring about adaptive change. Seeing their existing culture clearly through an analysis of everyday language can be a transformative step in achieving such change.

Approaching culture through the language an organisation uses, repeatedly and habitually, without thinking and on a daily basis, provides a systematic and rigorous way to surface the unspoken but powerful rules that guide what everyone is doing. Once the current rules are surfaced, they can be discussed and evaluated in the light of current objectives; from a new shared understanding strategic change can be achieved. Analysis of a shared language can easily be explained and made transparent to its speakers; implications and outcomes are also accessible and can be exciting and energising for people at all levels.

In this chapter, I will outline the practical and theoretical roots of this method and share examples of its application drawn from our experience with public, private and third sector organisations in the UK and the USA.

Why internal language matters to organisations

Origins

Two observations and some academic investigation laid the foundations of the consulting model outlined here. As a commercial consumer researcher in the UK in the 1990s, I observed – and was increasingly frustrated by – the way even large and sophisticated client organisations appeared to create and re-create the same problems. They would try to solve essentially the same issue, or develop the same apparent opportunity, every few years with new consumer research. This generated good business for a trusted research supplier, but was puzzling and clearly wasteful.

At the same time, I became intensely interested in the way those client organisations *talked*. In briefing meetings with, for example, packaged-goods marketers talking about food and cooking, or financial service providers talking about people and credit cards, I would listen and marvel at the interesting planets they lived on. Each one was perfectly formed; it contained solid-sounding concepts, clear ideas and coherent logical connections. This integrated system of language and ideas was treated as real, true, obvious and useful. But I knew the world it described or assumed was not the same as the one inhabited by those people I was about to interview. The organisation didn't simply use peculiar terms for everyday ideas and objects; rather, they seemed to carve the world up into quite different categories – to see it in a fundamentally different way from 'lay' people. Some 'technical' constructs – *value proposition, reason to believe (RTB), benefit* – clearly functioned as the currency of parts of the organisation. But beyond this there would be 'everyday' concepts – say *convenience food* or *luxury* or *value for money* – that also appeared to have a unique, specific meaning within the discourse of the company.

The job of a commercial researcher is to bridge this divide – to bring the sense-making strategies and worldview of the consumer into the world of the client. But it felt like there was something concrete about the client's organisational language – it had real, material effects. Importantly, it seemed to be stopping those organisations from hearing what consumer research was regularly telling them. Insights recognised by the client as valuable at the time of presentation were not being absorbed and used much beyond that moment, and it seemed to me that the client's internal language system was implicated.

A quest for answers led to a rich store of academic theory and method – 'discourse analysis' and related approaches. A wide-ranging set of ideas and tools for analysing language systematically offered a possible solution to earlier frustrations. So I set out in 2002 to develop methods for applying discourse and linguistic theory pragmatically to business and organisational problems – to explore how the material effects of language could be exposed, and this knowledge used to help make organisations more effective. The framework for thinking, which is the subject of this chapter and which shapes our work at Linguistic Landscapes, came from the decade of experimentation and application that followed.

Language shapes thought and action

I will assert through this chapter that an organisation's culture is reflected and held in place by habitual surface language, and that both culture and language have real, tangible consequences for its success. You might think that the language used internally by an organisation – rather than in its external communications – doesn't matter that much. This section outlines why it matters a great deal.

Language is far from trivial; it 'constructs' reality at a shared cultural level, building and sustaining things like social structures, power rela- tionships and 'truths', all of which have material consequences. A small illustration: some years ago in the UK, previously uncoined terms began to appear in public discourse to describe a set of experiences, including chronic extreme tiredness and joint pain, being reported by increasing numbers of people. The phenomenon became known, depending on context, as 'Yuppie Flu'; or 'Myalgic Encephalopathy' (later 'ME'). The first term belongs to a tabloid discourse of cynical mockery; the second draws firmly on the discourse of science and medicine. What happened to someone with this experience – socially, financially and physically – was hugely influenced by the name and frame their experience was given. On the one hand they were laughed at or ignored, and on the other they were taken seriously, treated as sick and given medical therapy. Language matters, because it affects what happens to people.

Internal organisational language is similarly material; it is implicated in what can be done, thought and heard by those within the enterprise; it affects what happens, what is valued, and what gets treated as 'true'.

Let's look briefly at some theory and evidence. Essentially my position is constructivist: that language shapes or guides thought, it is hard for anyone to think the unsayable, and that language constructs social reality; it 'brings things into being'. The philosophical details of social constructivism and constructionism are beyond the scope of this chapter (see e.g. Berger and Luckman 1966, Searle 1995), but Phillips and Hardy (2002) offer a definition of discourse which indicates the potentially enormous implications of seeing language in this way:

> We define a discourse as an interrelated set of texts, and the practices of their production, dissemination and reception, that brings an object into being. For example, the collection of texts of various kinds that make up the discourse of psychiatry brought the idea of the unconscious into existence in the 19th century (Foucault 1965). In other words, social reality is produced and made real through discourse, and social interactions cannot be fully understood without reference to the discourses that give them meaning.
>
> (2002: 3)

Here's another more trivial but familiar example: in the UK and the USA in 2012, the idea of 'detoxing' our bodies is real in that it has a social and economic reality; there is a financially significant industry in detoxing foods, detoxing vitamin supplements and detoxing health spa treatments. Physical detoxing is also secure enough as a construct to be used metaphorically and transferred to other things – we talk about detoxing our lives, or our relationships. But according to Google's NGram viewer (http://books.google.com/ngrams), the word detox barely appeared at all in English books before 1970 and did not really take off until around 1980, after which its use rocketed. Was there no such thing as 'detoxing' before 1970? What did we do about our toxins? Is detoxing 'real' and 'true' – or is it a social construct? I would argue it is both; they are inseparable.

In addition to the constructivist argument, which has a social or cultural focus, there is a long-running linguistic debate about how far habitual language shapes individual thought. Many will be familiar with the Sapir–Whorf hypothesis, which suggests that specific languages effectively enable and limit certain kinds of thought. Parts of the original work are now discredited, but Deutscher's recent and careful review of evidence concludes that 'the concepts we are trained to treat as distinct, the information our mother tongue continuously forces us to specify, the details it requires us to be attentive to, and the repeated associations it imposes on us' (2011: 234) do indeed have a role in shaping habits of mind. Boroditsky's work in cognitive psychology also leads her to conclude:

> Studies have shown that changing how people speak changes how they think. Teaching people new colour words, for instance, changes their ability to discriminate colours. And teaching people a new way of talking about time gives them a new way of thinking about it.
>
> (2011: 65)

While Deutscher's focus is on habits within one's mother tongue, and Boroditsky's on experimental manipulations, our practical experience indicates that the influence of language on thought applies in some form to habitual organisational discourse.

In organisations, language makes certain things happen and stops other things from happening. One client – a government agency – had operated for many years with a fixed binary categorisation of its users. While not a formal segmentation, a specific and well-used internal phrase constantly divided customers into two groups; in essence they were either good or bad; angels or devils; cooperative or uncooperative. The linguistic distinction was found everywhere, from business objectives to departmental titles to informal conversation, and was linked to a somewhat aggressive internal discourse. However, there was an embryonic competing discourse that suggested things were not that simple – it replaced the simple moral (good/bad) distinction with a more complex one. Maybe some people were less cooperative not because they were bad, but because they were confused? Maybe the agency needed to engage differently with those people? Over time, the agency developed a formal segmentation of users which was more complex than the old informal one – five separately named segments instead of two – and this new internal language helped create the space for more subtle, variable and *effective* forms of customer engagement. Actions and language were closely linked – new customer categories did not themselves change staff behaviour, but the revised engagement strategy would have been harder to sustain without the clear category names which supported it and which challenged the 'old' informal classification. This and other internal behaviour change was also arguably supported by the internally shocking insight into the existing culture that the original analysis provided.

Deutscher (2011) additionally argues that language shapes thought not through what *can* be but through what *must* be said. Some languages require the speaker to specify the gender of inanimate as well as animate objects, while in others neutrality is available; this has been shown to have subtle but significant effects on perception of those objects.

In an organisational context, categories exist that *must* be filled – things to which attention *must* be paid. Organisational constructs like 'initiatives', 'campaigns', 'strategies' or 'policies' are not just theoretical or abstract categories – they organise behaviour, attract budget, provide the means of exercising power and allow or block certain kinds of action. They are items of barter and trade in the organisational economy; instruments of status and distinction in the social system of the organisation. For example, some years ago it would have been hard to get more than a small part of the marketing budget to develop a website, even in a large company – but now the 'Digital Team' delivering the 'Digital Strategy' (note how these have acquired capitalised titles) most likely attracts substantial budget, staff and status.

Other categories exert power in an organisation because they are part of systems of control and management of the business. Within a marketing discourse, for example, the category *'reason to believe'* or 'RTB' is often one which literally requires filling (e.g. on an advertising brief) when defining a consumer proposition. This is fine – but it embeds a particular set of assumptions about how people make brand decisions, and thus legitimises and reinforces a certain approach to customers. This approach may over time become less useful or outdated, but it is 'baked in' to the internal discourse and is therefore hard to shift.

You might argue that most organisations hire smart people who are independent and able to make their own choices about how to think and talk. Shared habitual language acts like a well-trodden path. It is not that you can't strike out across the long grass, but most people don't. It is not only easier to go the familiar way, but if people thought about it at all, they would assume that the path must be there for a reason – that it goes somewhere useful. And of course mostly none of us do think about it, because we tend to feel that language is just the means through which we express ideas that somehow exist elsewhere. There is convincing evidence that this is not the case.

So, if language makes things happen and brings things into being, how then can we analyse language in organisations in a way that gives access to its constructive force?

Analysing discourse – accessing the constructive nature of language

An exciting range of theory and method has emerged over the past two decades that allows close examination of language and its effects. The focus is not on how language works grammatically, nor on what language means in a dictionary sense, but on how it works *in practice, in the world*. That is, it focuses on the social and cultural meanings it encodes, the social actions it performs, the relationships it assumes and the 'truths' it perpetuates. These methods arose across a wide range of disciplines, especially psychology, sociology and sociolinguistics, and are now in widespread use in academia. They hold a distinct perspective on language and its function in human experience and culture, connecting the micro (specific features of language use) with the macro (cultural and social meaning and action).

These academic paradigms provide strong building blocks for applied practice, and we use multiple frameworks developed from this array. Important specific sources within our own practice include Critical Discourse Analysis (CDA); Conversation Analysis (CA); Foucauldian analysis; discursive psychology; cognitive linguistics and systemic functional linguistics. We make use of quantitative methods (known as corpus linguistics) where useful but the research work is largely qualitative.

These approaches vary greatly, but they tend to share some core principles, the most fundamental of which is that language is action. So, saying is not the *opposite* of doing; saying *is* doing. Generally, we think of language as a neutral and transparent medium through which we access and describe real things. So people tend to regard language (e.g. what people say in interviews, or the text of a company report) as a way to find out more about topics or realities we are interested in – what consumers think and feel about a brand, or how well a company has done this year and how it plans to grow its business. A constructivist view of language treats it not as a route or window leading to the 'reality' of the topic of study, but as a significant and productive topic of study in itself (Tonkiss 1998, Phillips and Hardy 2002, Wood and Kroger 2000). Seen this way, language can reveal quite different things, such as the way the consumer 'manages' their self-presentation and identity in relation to this brand in the social setting of the focus group or the way the company report constructs its (perhaps controversial) decisions as rational and inevitable. In this way, language can be analysed as a social practice, implicated in the establishment and maintenance of particular truths and relationships – especially of power – that are otherwise hard to identify or articulate (Potter and Wetherell 1987, Wood and Kroger 2000, Fairclough 2001).

There is immense richness offered by these schools of thought, and one can use a complex range of both discursive features and conceptual frameworks as a resource. In applied work informed eclecticism is not just acceptable but is essential; we must look for whatever helps make sense of a situation and for insight that will help the client organisation solve the issues it faces. Methodological eclecticism and pragmatism do not mean we can ignore issues of validity and quality though, so applied practice also means developing bespoke and context-appropriate ways to address these issues, to underpin a professional practice based on systematic analysis.

Putting it into practice

If language is not a transparent medium through which we talk and write about a fixed reality, but instead constructs that reality, we can regard an organisation's habitual discourse as creating and re-creating a coherent but idiosyncratic conceptual model of the world – building and sustaining a particular kind of reality.

In practice, we take 'discourse' to mean the nature and structure of language within sets of spoken or written texts (often the everyday operational language of Company X) *and* the web of assumption, implicit reference and implication that sits beneath or around that language and which gives it meaning in practice (the taken-for-granted and unspoken truths within Company X about 'who we are, what we do and what matters around here'). At its simplest, analysis of discourse gives a way of 'reversing into' shared assumptions and frames of reference – working out what must be there, crucial to meaning but always unspoken, for observable surface language to make sense. So we analyse surface language to generate a hypothesis about silent working assumptions.

We access the discourse of an organisation through forensic examination of its verbal language (as opposed to other data such as spaces, décor, body posture, gesture, etc. which are also rich sources but which require different kinds of engagement). Language has two properties that are relevant to its role in revealing organisational culture: first, language, like culture, 'gets everywhere', and second, language becomes familiar and therefore invisible to those for whom it is most important. The first means that language offers an efficient and objective way to sample culture and the second that it is hard to access by those on the inside. We will now look a little closer at each of these.

Language and culture are everywhere

Other analysts of organisational culture do not of course ignore language. Methods such as ethnography, or workshop processes used to 'map' corporate culture (Schein 1999, 2004, Johnson 1992, Johnson et al. 2011), also aim to make the implicit explicit, and these do pay attention to linguistic forms, such as stories, or to managerial discourse. Watson (2001), for example, uses ideas from Foucault and others and offers this elegant and simple definition of discourse:

> A connected set of statements, concepts, terms and expressions which constitutes a way of talking and writing about a particular issue, thus framing the way people understand and act with respect to that issue.
>
> (2001: 113)

There is also a body of academic work applying discursive approaches to organisation studies (Grant et al. 2004), including studying organisations through specific linguistic notions – notably metaphor (Cornelisson et al. 2008, Oswick and Grant 1996).

The question we set out to address is how to use the broad idea of discourse, and the widest variety of analytic tools available, to tackle concrete problems of strategic development, culture and change and to do so effectively, efficiently and at scale. Analysing everyday language, including that not normally regarded as data, is a particular – and in our experience highly effective – way to map culture. This is because culturally specific language choices are visible in all spheres and aspects of an organisation; its structure (in divisional names and job titles); its processes (in process names and shorthand); and its people and their everyday interactions. Language both absorbs and constantly reflects the unspoken culture – and in doing so perpetuates it and makes it 'sticky'. We can regard language as culture-in-action; culture and language are inextricably connected and culture shows up at all sites and functions in an organisation – it gets into the water supply. So, for practical purposes, sampling *language* widely across different kinds of 'texts' allows one to pick up and illustrate a pervasive set of *cultural* truths.

An example may help here: a financial services client had a culture in which (among other things) regulation and authority ruled. Regulation-talk (heavy use of 'ought/should/must'; frequent references to the regulatory authority; a control-related lexicon) littered every internal conversation and found its way into every crevice of the business. We noticed, for example, that the place where customer application forms were scanned was called the 'DCU' or 'Document Control Unit'. It didn't actually *control* them, it just *scanned* them. But notions of regulation and control were culturally important, and at some time someone had decided that's what it should be called. Intense focus on formal control and authority had at one time been strategically appropriate and commercially effective, but was now fighting against a strategic need and indeed desire for increased focus on consumers and a more contemporary and less officious approach. On one level, this specific scrap of language – the 'Document Control Unit' – might not seem to matter; it was just a name for a department. But on another level, as part of a constellation of small and large examples, it served to perpetuate a culture that was once useful and appropriate, but was now undermining strategic objectives.

Language becomes invisible to those it affects most

If linguistic clues to culture are everywhere, why does it need specialised analysis to bring organisational language and its implications into view?

When people first join a new organisation, for the first few weeks or months they can 'hear' the way it speaks. Even if the new company operates in the same sector as the last, it sounds subtly and curiously different. There might be new acronyms and unfamiliar jargon, but that's not the biggest issue. People are actually talking in a weirdly different way. They may refer to processes or customer groups strangely, highlight unexpected things and ignore what the previous employer treated as fundamental. The new employee begins to realise that this new organisation understands the world differently; it uses unfamiliar maps, even of a familiar landscape. It operates with a fundamentally different worldview from the one they just left. When we share this 'first-few-weeks' observation with staff at any level, in any kind of organisation, there are nods of agreement. Everyone remembers how that felt.

The language the new employee 'hears' in those early days provides clues through which they begin to understand – only semi-consciously, and pretty rapidly, if they are to survive and thrive – the unspoken culture of the organisation. Things like:

- *who we are*
- *who those people are 'out there' (customers, audiences or users and other key groups like competitors, shareholders or regulators)*
- *what we think of them*
- *what the relationship is between us*
- *what really matters round here*
- *what we are really here to do.*

This view of language bears a clear relationship to Schein's work on 'levels of culture' (1999, 2004). He describes three levels, from the easily visible to the hidden: (i) 'artifacts' (visible structures, processes and behaviour – easy to see but hard to decipher) (ii) 'espoused beliefs and values' (ideals, aspirations and ideologies – may not match behaviour) and (iii) 'underlying assumptions' (unconscious, taken-for-granted beliefs and values – determine behaviour but are hard to see).

We think about visible and hidden aspects of culture in this way:

Surface language: Everyday organisational language habits and conventions – spoken and written, formal and informal language at all levels and in all business areas.
Claims and wishes: Public statements of vision, mission and values; plus conscious accounts and explanations of how and why things are the way they are.

Silent assumptions: Unspoken rules of thumb about 'who we are, what we do and how we do it', governing actions and decisions below the level of conscious thought.

Systematic, forensic analysis of the two kinds of visible language – everyday language, plus public declarations, explanations and accounts – suggests what sits at the silent, unspoken level. So we can say 'From the way you talk around here, the evidence suggests this is what you assume to be true – about yourselves, about customers, about your purpose as an organisation'. This is not the end but the beginning of a conversation – if it is to be useful, this hypothesis needs to be interrogated, developed and assimilated by the organisation itself.

The 'silent assumptions' are quite literally the unspokens that colour everything the organisation does and which help to keep it recognisably the same organism, even as people join and leave. The internal *discourse* of an organisation gives clues to the implicit rules of thumb that govern actions and decisions, usually below the level of conscious or critical thought. It might contain simple but powerful notions like 'we must never offend anyone' or 'customers are dangerous and we must keep them out'. These ideas – the examples are from real projects – have tangible effects. The 'don't offend' culture led to inaction where action was clearly needed (this was a campaigning charity – offending a few people was likely to be inevitable if the organisation was doing its job well). The 'customers are dangerous and we must keep them out' culture was implicated, unsurprisingly, in devastatingly bad customer service and satisfaction levels, both of which had serious implications for the business involved.

The existence of a specific organisational culture embedded in language is at its most tangible to new joiners because that language is unfamiliar to them – but this unfamiliarity will only last for a while. After a few months they will have learned the language and absorbed the culture – they will be talking like old-timers and operating effortlessly within the rules of thumb and taken-for-granted truths embedded within that language.

Note that the only person likely to be in a position seriously to *question* the silent assumptions – assuming they 'hear' them while the language is still unfamiliar to them – is a new Chief Executive Officer (CEO). Everyone else is more likely to be learning rapidly how to operate in this new world and get on with the job they have been hired to do. In fact it can be helpful for an incoming CEO or Chief Operations Officer (COO) to have an early discourse review – even at a small scale; a discreet and objective reading of the unspoken culture of the company allows the new leader to consider its implications for their strategic and personal objectives.

It is true that some people always 'hear' (and often criticise) the language of their employer; they retain some sense of its strangeness and they can hear its subtext or implication. Some of these corporate mavericks will be heard – but others will be side-lined until there is some more general desire to change, and/or a collective sense that 'there's something unhelpful about our language'.

Language and culture change

Organisational language matters to those developing strategy and to those interested in encouraging change. It matters because both silent assumptions *and* surface language tend to hang around long after the worldview they entail has ceased to be adaptive and useful – *because nobody can articulate the unspokens, by definition, and no one can 'hear' the implications of the surface language because it is too familiar.* Silent assumptions contain gems that are long-term assets – but they can also act as a powerful brake on change, even where the organisation as a whole wants and believes that it needs such a change.

In a 'top–down' model of strategy development, typically, a market or operating environment changes and a new strategy is developed and announced. But if the unspokens are not surfaced and challenged, or re-worked and integrated into the new strategic direction, supported by relevant changes to habitual language, then little changes. The old stability is simply disrupted and there is fracture and instability, as managers try to push through a change that it is quite literally impossible for the organisation to make sense of, believe in, talk about and operationalise within its current discourse.

More positively, there might be embedded in language the traces of hidden or forgotten assets (e.g. a deep commitment to careful evaluation of evidence) that have been present for a long time but which need surfacing and celebrating for their continuing value to the organisation in times of change.

Either way, these silent assumptions tend to be highly stable, espe-cially if they remain silent and unacknowledged. As Schein describes:

> Basic assumptions... tend to be nonconfrontable and nondebatable and hence are extremely difficult to change. To learn something new in this realm requires us to resurrect, reexamine and possibly change some of the more stable portions of our cognitive structure.
>
> (2004: 31)

Today's 'silent' thinking – and the habitual language that both reflects and holds it in place – was once useful and fully adapted to past market conditions. Today's organisational culture is, as Schein also sug-gests, the product of past success – a sedimented 'reality' now invisibly accepted as natural, true and inevitable.

This view of internal discourse might be described as strategy-as-language; strategy is formed and re-formed day to day in the everyday interactions of everyone in the business. In this, a degree of stability is good and helpful. Shared shorthand helps everyone get on with the job; and linguistic stability is part of an organi-sational stability that is useful for other reasons too. But language can become out of step – it might end up being the most inflexible practice in the organisation, and because it operates below conscious-ness, its dragging effect might not be noticed. Outdated strategic intents and patterns of thinking become locked or encoded into long-established routine language, common shorthand and 'insider' language, and further fixed by even less dynamic cultural ele-ments such as job titles, departmental titles and the official names of objects and processes. The language/thinking connections that were once useful may have become 'core rigidities' (Leonard-Barton 1992).

Using language to help change

What happens when one makes cultural unspokens widely visible in an organisation? In our practice, we emphasise that we are interested in language at the collective level, not in blaming or criticising anyone – and that good as well as less good is buried here. We note that shared expectations about ways to behave and make decisions are embedded in the way of talking that everyone learned when they joined. And as the analysis begins to show people something really new in what has been under their noses for so long, there is usually a collective 'aha!' or 'doh!' moment. It often articulates something which people have sensed or struggled with, but not had a vocabulary with which to talk about.

Importantly, this insight is itself an intervention – it brings change and often a significant release of energy as people suddenly see new ways to act and think. This can be very exciting, both for those involved and for us as consultants. Recently, we worked with a charity which had become muddled about its core purpose, at a deep level. In well-intentioned efforts to be more inclusive, it had blurred its focus and lost sight of the person for whom it really existed. We showed them how this played out persistently in internal and indeed external language. Without further intervention, and with renewed vigour, many individuals and teams reported that they had immediately started to refocus in language and action on 'the person who matters'.

Leaders can inadvertently sustain an 'old' culture, even when committed intellectually to change, so one can work with senior teams to help them understand how their leadership language intersects with the habitual language of the organisation. Working with the senior management team of a large public sector organisation, we played back a number of pervasive features of their language: a hyper-politeness that occasionally leaked a Rottweiler aggression; a distinctly gendered dismissal of a 'customer focus' project ('pink and fluffy'; the 'cuddly customer thing') and more. They were dismayed – but they then had the power to act differently if they chose. Our objective was not to judge or criticise but to reflect; it is almost impossible to 'hear' your own language, but once you do, the knowledge is yours to use. Holding a mirror up, allowing people across the organisation to 'see' the silent assumptions that constitute their own shared culture, can be catalytic in enabling such shifts in understanding.

Although the insight offered by language analysis can be visibly transformative, one cannot naïvely ignore issues such as the anxiety, defensiveness or destabilisation that surfacing cultural assumptions can bring. Focusing the work on *shared* language and on *learned* behaviour seems to deflect some of this – people may be anxious about change, but when they see for themselves the systematic way in which the existing culture operates, they can take part in collective work to consider its continued usefulness into the future. In practice this is less effective if framed as getting 'buy-in' to the idea of change (see e.g. Kotter 1995). It is in fact more effective when seen as providing *feedback* into a complex social system – allowing the system to know itself better and adjust to a changing environment. Shared insight helps people at all levels to make sense of what they often already feel – that 'things don't work well any more around here' and that change is needed.

Nor can we ignore the issue of power. We may see a hardening and defending of entrenched positions as the analysis uncovers how the status quo – the hegemony – is held in place. While flushing this out may be uncomfortable, it shifts the terms of the debate away from specifics or details of change and onto the really important issues – *who we are, what we do, what our relationship is to the outside world* – and to points of conflict at this level.

What about introducing new language? Will this make everyone think and behave differently? Language alone cannot bring about cultural change, but it can be a powerful intervention to *help* in a change process. In practice, we often help an organisation formulate a new set of silent assumptions for themselves – to articulate 'how we would need to be' to support a given strategy. Temporarily surfaced and spoken whilst people practice and adjust, over time these revised silent assumptions should indeed become silent again – settling into the essence of an adjusted and evolved culture. The transition needs support through a set of working principles, and small amounts of deliberate language change (job or department titles, or key instruments like widely used forms) to help *remind* everyone 'how it is we want to be in relation to customers/users'. Such visible linguistic beacons temporarily disrupt the normal invisibility of shared language, and pin new thinking in place while other forms of change, engagement or collective adjustment can take place.

Beyond change: internal discourse matters in other ways

Our primary focus is on language as a route to *organisational strategic insight* and understanding, not on language as a product or output. Language 'products' may flow from it – better staff or customer communications, or more effective advertising – but we are most interested in what a close analysis of language offers for other objectives such as strategic management and culture change.

However, we see that internal discourse inevitably leaks out – that it *flows*. Internal silent assumptions are reflected in what customers or other audiences see on the outside, even if subtly. This is not a question of letting 'expert talk' or jargon cross into consumer-facing materials; it is leakage of more subtle, embedded assumptions, often about the way the organisation sees customers or other stakeholders and its relationship with them.

One organisation we worked with, for example, had at root a fundamental disrespect for its customers. They were regarded as stupid, unable to understand the financial products they had bought and ultimately culpable for that lack of understanding. This was rarely said so brutally, but was implied consistently in its internal discourse – and it leaked through the company's communications, which were seen by customers as authoritative but unfriendly, confusing and off-putting. Apart from ethical objection to a powerful institution regarding customers as stupid, even if subtly, the key competitors in the market at the time were combining authority with friendliness and ease of access, and disrespect was a commercially dangerous position to take.

Another company operated with a respectful but transactional view of customers – their internal discourse constructed customers as largely rational users of their services. Comparative analysis of consumer discourse showed that, unusually, existing customers used the language of intimate and long-term relationships and constructed their relationship with the brand as exactly that – a meaningful relationship. They expected the brand to honour the bond they felt they had, and much negative customer feedback was explicable once this framing was understood and explained. A set of working principles was developed cooperatively and used to guide both language and business decisions across the organisation. A positive increase in performance on business metrics resulted, including better retention of customers and significant improvement on key indicators such as Net Promoter Score. So one can certainly combine insight about cultural issues (clear understanding of reasons for existing engrained problems) with practical outcomes (e.g. better contact with customers, more effective internal conversations/effective working and improvement on quantified metrics).

How and why does internal discourse interact with other discourses? This is our working model:

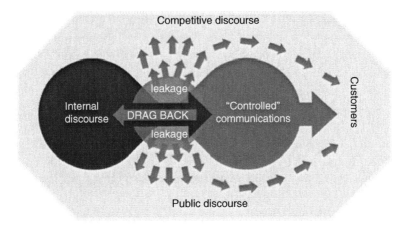

The internal taken-for-granted leaks out through external 'controlled' communications like advertising and web material, even when good external agencies are engaged. It happens for two reasons. First, because agencies need to develop close client relationships, inevitably they absorb the client's own discourse over time and start to speak and think like them. It also happens because the sign-off process (e.g. for advertising) suffers from 'drag-back' – the agency might build a new idea based on an entirely fresh set of assumptions about how the brand or company relates to customers (say, designed to meet changed customer needs), but the organisation cannot feel comfortable with it and either rejects it wholesale or dilutes and drags it back to something closer to the existing norm.

Internal discourse also leaks through non-controlled sources of contact with customers and indeed other stakeholders; via staff who have external contact but who are not in 'controlled' areas like communications, brand, marketing or sales. Contact may be voice, e-mail, letter or face to face, but it does not go through the same channels – the line between 'inside' and 'outside' may be very thin indeed.

Summing up

Language becomes invisible when it is familiar, yet it shapes, guides and constrains our thinking. An organisation's internal language shapes and enables certain forms of thinking and modes of action. It may remain fixed even as other practices change and as such it can create a kind of stickiness. Some of this stickiness creates stability and helps retain a consistent identity; some can problematically fossilise a strategy and way of being that was once adaptive and successful but has ceased to be so. Analysing internal language with tools offered by discourse analysis, linguistics and associated methods offers a powerful option for organisations engaged in strategic development, and especially in innovation and strategic change. It is powerful because it brings to visibility and therefore to conscious consideration that most ethereal but foundational object in an organisation – its culture.

What can this approach offer an organisation? And how is it different from what has so far been available?

- The method accesses and reveals organisational culture through systematic and theoretically grounded methods.
- Findings can be well illustrated with examples from the familiar language that surrounds people every day and, although based on technical analysis, can easily be expressed in non-technical terms. Findings are rich and interesting, so they make sense and are engaging to people at all levels.
- The work is powerfully self-validating – people recognise their own culture instantly. They have felt its effects, but have often not been able to grasp it, nor had the vocabulary with which to talk about or question it before.
- It is energetically positive; there is often a palpable release and rush of energy as people realise the implications of what they are seeing. Shifts in language and behaviour can sometimes come about without further intervention as the 'system' re-organises around new knowledge.
- Culture permeates all the pores of the organisation and language absorbs as well as perpetuates the unspoken assumptions of the culture, expressing it all through the organisation. So it is possible to collect enough data to provide a good reading of the culture, for sharing and development with the organisation itself, through qualitative sampling of texts. This means it is practical to carry out a useful project at a scale that is not prohibitive, and if necessary this can be done at speed.

- It is not invasive or disruptive as a process, nor threatening to individuals if explained well, with an emphasis on the shared nature of culture and shared language.

This method can be used early in planning or starting a process of change, or as a 'remedial' intervention where change is under way but proving difficult and slow to implement. Reviewing language and being aware of its power gives leaders a tangible way to work with culture, to harness its beneficial relevance to the current context and to evolve away from its less beneficial or outdated aspects. It can also heighten awareness of the role of leadership language in the introduction and implementation of new strategy or strategic intent. Longer term, being aware of and auditing its own language helps an organisation become more efficient, open and adaptive to changing conditions.

Culture is one of the most commonly talked about managerial and leadership issues in organisations, but few take steps to engage with culture actively and strategically, not least because it has been difficult to do so. Understanding the connection between an organisation's language and the way its people think, act and perform gives a concrete and grounded route to accessing and engaging with this important and powerful phenomenon.

References

Berger, P. and Luckmann, T. (1966). *The Social Construction of Reality: A Treatise in the Sociology of Knowledge*, London: Penguin.

Boroditsky, L. (2011). 'How Language Shapes Thought'. *Scientific American*, February: 63–65. Available at: http://www.scientificamerican.com/article. cfm?id=how-language-shapes-thought.

Cornelisson, J., Oswick, C., Christensen, L. and Phillips, N. (2008). 'Metaphor in Organizational Research: Context, Modalities and Implications for Research – Introduction'. *Organization Studies* 29(01): 7–22.

Deal, T. and Kennedy, A. (1982). *Corporate Cultures: The Rites and Rituals of Corporate Life*, London: Penguin.

Deutscher, G. (2011). *Through the Language Glass: Why the World Looks Different in Other Languages*, London: Arrow Books.

Fairclough, N. (2001). *Language and Power* 2nd ed., Harlow Essex: Pearson Education.

Foucault, M. (1965). *Madness and Civilization: A History of Insanity in the Age of Reason*, New York: Vintage.

Grant, D., Keenoy, T. and Oswick, C. (1998). *Discourse+Organization*, London: Sage.

Grant, D., Hardy, C., Oswick, C. and Putnam, L. (2004). *The Sage Handbook of Organizational Discourse*, London: Sage.

Jaruzelski, B., Loehr, J. and Holman, R. (2011). 'The Global Innovation 1000: Why Culture is Key'. *Strategy+Business magazine* (65), Winter: 1–16. Available at: http://www.strategy-business.com/article/11404.

Johnson, G. (1992). 'Managing Strategic Change – Strategy, Culture and Action'. *Long Range Planning* 25(1): 28–36.

Johnson, G., Whittington, R. and Scholes, K. (2011). *Exploring Strategy* 9th ed., Harlow Essex: Pearson Education.

Kotter, J.P. (1995). 'Leading Change: Why Transformation Efforts Fail'. *Harvard Business Review* 75(2): 59–67.

Leonard-Barton, D. (1992). 'Core Capabilities and Core Rigidities: A Paradox in Managing New Product'. *Strategic Management Journal* 13(S1), Summer: 111–125.

Oswick, C. and Grant, D. (1996). *Organisation Development: Metaphorical Explorations*, London: Pearson Education.

Phillips, N. and Hardy, C. (2002). *Discourse Analysis: Investigating Processes of Social Construction.* Sage University Papers Series on Qualitative Research Methods, Vol. 50. Thousand Oaks, CA, Sage.

Potter, J. and Wetherell, M. (1987). *Discourse and Social Psychology: Beyond Attitudes and Behaviour*, London: Sage.

Schein, E.H. (1999). *The Corporate Culture Survival Guide*, San Francisco, CA: Jossey-Bass.

Schein, E.H. (2004). *Organizational Culture and Leadership*, San Francisco, CA: Jossey-Bass.

Searle, J.R. (1995). *The Construction of Social Reality*, London: Penguin.

Tonkiss, F. (1998). Analysing Discourse, in C. Seale (ed.), *Researching Society and Culture*, London: Sage.

Watson, T.J. (2001). *In Search of Management: Culture, Chaos and Control in Managerial Work*, London: Thomson Learning.

Wood, L.A. and Kroger, R.O. (2000). *Doing Discourse Analysis: Methods for Studying Action in Talk and Text*, Thousand Oaks, CA: Sage.

9
Strategy as Serious Play

Julie Verity and Lewis Pinault

To my observation, in over 10 years and more than a thousand workshops using hands-on construction toys like LEGO, 3-D brick-based methods are unmatched for their ability to allow people to build rich, complex and systematic views of their professional challenges, and are as yet an unbottomed means of sounding new depths of creativity, innovation and strategic foresight.

These are the words of Lewis Pinault, author of the *Play Zone* (Pinault 2004), the Senior Director of *Serious Play for Business* in 2008, founder of Box Exchange[1] and visitor on our Cass Executive MBA programmes. Throughout this chapter, he will share his rich experience of the serious play technique. Lewis worked with Professors Johan Roos and Bart Victor of the international business school IMD, who were championed by Kjel Kristiansen the family owner of the LEGO Company to develop the serious play technique as a superior team-building, learning and strategy-making tool. These two academics were intrigued by two fundamental ideas:

(i) if the strategy-making process changed, would the content generated also change?
(ii) and if so, could it be a superior outcome?

They were handed the perfect opportunity to indulge their curiosity when asked to design an executive learning programme for the LEGO Company. Leaders at LEGO had a deep interest and knowledge about the learning benefits of play but had never thought to explore its potential in the hands of grown-ups and for the purpose of organisational learning and strategy-making. But, they were very supportive of the idea, and over the two years that the programme ran, Victor and Roos explored how model-building, storytelling, creating metaphor and working in three-dimensions(3D), that is 'playing', might substitute as a strategy and learning process for the two-dimensional (2D) conversational process that is conventional business practice.

That was in the late nineties. Since then, serious play has proved its potential as a technique with a solid theoretical grounding and practitioner endorsement as a tool that has many benefits over conventional strategy processes, demonstrating consistently different and superior outcomes. So, yes, if the strategy-making process is 3D, playful and follows a few pre-specified rules, what emerges are (i) more imaginative outcomes, (ii) insights and shared understanding are achieved faster, (iii) complexity and ambiguity are accommodated more effectively, (iv) commitment is won more easily and more deeply, (v) outcomes are more memorable and have a smoother path to making them happen.

This results in better strategy.

Can you imagine?

It can be unsettling. My first sight of serious play was a great mess of LEGO toys – thousands of them, drawn from every range of LEGO and combined by tens of pairs of hands – big Duplo blocks and panda bears and giraffes mixed up with standard 'system' bricks and human mini-figures of all descriptions and technical and robotics pieces: Jabba the Hut squeezed into a child's window, riding a motorised elephant, on top of a lagoon base, attacked by pirates and feeding on skeletons. Each element, I would find, had its own story, and was key to a broader narrative that told a total story, a story deftly revealing of the driving patterns and structures that underlay the real landscape of every participant's interactions.

It is unsettling to arrive for a strategy workshop or meeting and find toys heaped onto the middle of the boardroom table instead of the usual neat piles of power-point printouts, binders, consultants' reports and grey-leaded pencils. But, models and stories are not so unusual as vehicles for strategising (e.g. Jacobides 2010, Von Ghyczy 2003 and Snowden 2005). An ex-military officer, now one of our executive MBAs, made this vividly clear at a presentation he made to one of our Cass classes. In preparation for his class, James cleared the desks and gathered his audience onto the floor, dimmed the lights and played a short video. The screen displayed a desert landscape which, after a few seconds of silence, erupted into a maelstrom of what felt like men running and scrambling madly and chaotically through the shockingly loud noise of insistent, rattling crossfire from lethal hardware. This was a two-minute clip showing a Taliban hit squad clashing with a small US army scouting troop in Afghanistan.

The video ended. James reached for his coat and moulded it on the floor into the terrain that mimicked what was on the screen minutes earlier. He created small hills with scrunched-up sleeves and pockets jammed with rolled-up paper. He used his tie to indicate the rough track that ran along the valley bottom and placed discarded paper sandwich cartons on the valley sides where deserted concrete huts stood in reality. Paper cups from the coffee machine became probable enemy camps in hillside caves. A flip chart stand was placed due East as a symbol of the sun.

While constructing this landscape he described each part in a quiet, authoritative voice: 'This is the direction the sun will rise at precisely 06.20. It has to clear this small hill before it will begin to blind us as we move in this direction along the valley track. There are caves here and here. These have been used as Taliban hiding places in the past and there is space enough for ammunition to kill all of us. These buildings are potential places to take cover if we are ambushed. They are approximately X metres from the track, X seconds running time. Our destination is this point here and our task is to achieve this position etc...etc...'

Everyone listened with an intensity that is rare in class (!). When James finished, he replayed the video clip we saw earlier. It was the same clip, but the second seeing was a totally different experience. This time, there was a sense of the light changing as the sun rose. The buildings to the South were clearly visible whereas before none of the watchers had seen them. When the firing started, men ran in meaningful directions. There was a pattern and degrees of order, the perception of chaos disappeared. The video seemed longer, more details were discernable, the direction of the crossfire and the number of men injured could be seen clearly.

James' presentation was a combination of building a 3D model of the scene, describing it in metaphor, creating the atmosphere, incorporating the strategy and contingencies into the story and geography. Everything was together, contained within a story and 3D model. The senses of those in the class – sight, sound, imagination, fear – were heightened, all were intently bound-up in the experience. The strategy was set deep in the context and James created a clarity and aware-ness that two dimensions and flat bullet points could never have achieved.

Now, replace the military scene with a competitive business land-scape, replace paper coffee cups and a scrunched-up coat with LEGO bricks and figures, get the right stakeholders in the room and describe the organisational problem or goal and let serious play commence.

Getting serious about play

Some theory

The term 'serious play' was coined by Plato (1991) who philosophised about the difference between 'frivolous' and 'serious' play. He made a distinction between the two, (i) playing for fun and (ii) playing to achieve excellence in education. Roos et al. (2004) summarise:

> The term 'serious play' refers to the purpose and structure of philo-sophical dialogue in Platonic philosophy. The 'seriousness' pertains to the truth of the matter under consideration, while the 'play' per-tains to the movement of the dialectical method of questioning. Following Plato's argument, a seriously playful educational process can prepare individuals to contribute to a good society, and leaders to govern wisely.

How serious play differs from our more conventional means of making strategy is in the *medium* and the *mode*.

Usually, the medium of strategy is conversation and documentation. The conversation is about data, presented in spreadsheets, review docu-ments and research reports. Graphic tools are 2D abstractions of arrows on flowcharts, circles overlapping to form models and boxes arranged in orders on the page to signify market behaviours. Discussions about this documentation are usually made and shared in formal settings like meeting rooms, where the props are flipcharts and screens for viewing slide presentations.

The medium of serious play is 3D and LEGO elements offer an acces-sible, reusable, easily manipulated, rich set of elements that can be built up and joined together quickly.

The *mode* describes the sort of activities people in the debate are encouraged to participate in. Activities in a conventional strategy process are mostly cognitive, such as thinking about the data, analysing and assessing. The emphasis is on rational, logical thinking done in a mostly reflective and sedentary way. Together, the formal setting and the thinking, reflective approach, reduces the chance for experimentation, playful exploration, emergent and messy modes of group interaction. In comparison, serious play asks people to tell stories through metaphor after physically building a model. It offers the possibility of a richer experience by removing the constraints of formality and introducing the chance to be creative and imaginative and to use all the senses (Roos et al. 2004).

'Adults play to break from conventions, to experiment, to shift from normality into a rich world of imagination or to push themselves in new ways.

Play is becoming more accepted in business, where any tools and technologies that enable people to play with constraints and simulate alternative realities are seen as critical enablers of greater innovation' (The LEGO® Learning Institute 2011).

After two years of research with the LEGO Company, Johan Roos and his co-workers set up the Imagination lab where the work continued, winning sponsorship from (among others) Orange, Nokia, and Microsoft. LEGO also maintained their interest. Through this formal study, researchers consistently found that in the hands of managers LEGO bricks encouraged all the positive traits that any facilitator of a strategy process yearns for: great individual participation, high energy levels, rich conversations – broad and detailed, lots of information sharing, frequent laughter, animation. Participants had 'aha' moments, saying things like: 'I learned more about my colleagues' views today than during the whole of last year', and 'I have never seen it like this before.'

Lewis' experience

It definitely works. It strongly relates to the complexity sciences. What we are doing in a play workshop is to take a group of people with all of their ideas, their biases, their hopes and emotions, the things that are causing them anxiety, their knowledge and perceptions, and we make them interact in the proximity of the room. We speed the process with bricks, metaphor and story-telling and out of this emerges new pattern, new structure.

The bricks are very powerful. The colours can represent different things, there are human figures, chains, ladders, fences and animals. You can create rich, dense worlds.

We need to ensure that we have the right people in the room and the right number. If we constrain the system too strongly, with too many people or the wrong mix, that is without voices of authority on a subject or without the right knowledge, nothing new will emerge. But if we have enough to allow movement and we have diversity of perspective and knowledge, new ideas will emerge. That is the magic – new pattern and structure emerge from the interaction.

If you ask someone to place themselves into the model, then when you have a conversation to the object it is still an authentic conversation. If you have built yourself and another person has built themselves in the model as well, then you are almost having a richer conversation, you are taking more risk, you are saying things into and through the model that you would not say in a normal conversation.

But it is not just you, there is your landscape, concrete things like technology, abstract things like society, trends and changes that might happen; people build emotions and feelings into their models. Often you are peeling away deeper levels of stuff.

The model is there on the table, and when you have described it, it remains; people feel less compelled to repeat a point that they feel is important, because it is always there…you can always point back to the model. This seems to help accommodate even more complexity into the model because once something is built, we can trust it to be there while we turn our attention to something else. Others can say, yes, we can see that – we are not taking away how you feel or what you see. It speeds the process. When we ask people to connect their models, it happens very quickly.

Stuff happens

In a play workshop, people are asked to model how they perceive a current strategic issue. When individual models are built, each person describes their model with a story, telling why this colour and this shape have been chosen and what reality each of these represent. Emotions and facts are combined, as in real life. Others question the models and this is when everyone becomes involved in the reason, for example, why this competitor is built as a very large, aggressive beast and why this one is small, further away and perhaps hidden behind a screen. Each individual's story reveals to the rest of the group how they see and understand the territory of the issue. Using metaphor rather than 'talking data' is known to introduce rich new understanding (Schön 1963, 1993).

Typically the next step is to combine individual models into one that the whole group can agree to. This requires negotiation around differences and points of contention. Talking 'to the model' depersonalises the story and helps overcome inhibitions as Lewis observes above. This is also a great leveller offering the possibility to make hierarchical differences irrelevant. The model as a focus, it being physically present, removes defensive behaviours and increases respectfulness in others (Statler et al. 2002).

Focusing on the model also appears to increase the effectiveness of negotiation about changing individual views. When there, in the 'flow' of the play, it seems relatively easy to incorporate additional information that any one individual might not have and to make links, comparisons and agree that yes, this is a fair representation of the competitive landscape or the terrain surrounding the issue.

Managers who have been involved in serious play workshops report a substantial difference to their understanding and emotional involvement with strategic outcomes. Counter-intuitively, one reason for this improved understanding was the extra complexity that could be built into the model compared with a flat, theoretical or text conceptualisation (Bürgi and Roos 2003).

Lewis' experience

Respecting the model is a ground rule. We ask that people don't touch other peoples' models without permission. We make clear that a person's model is valid; if that is the way a person sees the issue then it is their reality, their story and we accept that. It is hard not to be completely honest, the language of building yourself and what you do is hard to falsify. People commit to their model. The model generates respect from others. In fact the whole process is more respectful than any I have seen generated from a pen and flipchart. People often want to take their models home or they want to take photos – that is rare when you are working with paper and pencil.

One of the consistent, big take-aways from a play experience for individuals is what they learn about others. It might be difficult for the individuals to recognize any shift in their own perspective, or moderation of their own thoughts. This would only happen for a person with a lot of self-awareness, and might not be necessary. But, what individuals do take away is the 'ah ha!' of how other people see themselves and how they make sense of what they do and the issue at hand, their role, how these overlap or sometimes where there are gaping holes.

There is therapeutic value in working with the model. If you can find another channel through which to talk, it is much easier to resolve conflicts and – well – just be brave. Sometimes people don't talk because they are shy or because groups have rejected ideas in the past. It takes courage to speak up and speak up again. It is a courage-building exercise and strategy is about courage. It is about having anticipatory skills and having a stance. It is about beginning to see more about what another person intends and seeing more about their agency in a complex environment. A physical object – like a model – helps.

Hands-on learning

Serious play draws heavily on what most of us were privileged to experience naturally as children, but these are skills that most of us also let wane in favour of our later, lazier established brain wiring.

Some theory

Piaget (1971) was interested in child development and learning. At a very young age, children hear and see everything that their parents and carers do and say as the 'truth', that is the right and the only interpretation of the world. At this stage in their development, they have no contrary information or experience. These infant interpretations of their environments are gradually expanded as they engage in the wider world and have to assimilate additional or different 'truths' from other people. Through this process of: knowing and subsequently having to assimilate new knowledge, children build what Piaget labelled as 'knowledge structures'. He called this process *constructivism*, symbolising the way knowledge is acquired through building new experiences into an ever more sophisticated and complex mind model. Integral to constructivism was the notion that physically building things in the 'concrete' sense fed back into 'mind' knowledge creating a virtual circle of learning through a craft-like process.

Papert was one of Piaget's students. He believed that this method of learning was universal and applicable throughout life and not something that we grew out of with maturity. He argued, for example, that introducing appropriate 3D models into maths classes would help students learn mathematical concepts.[2] So a *constructionist* approach to learning is superior because of positive feedback loops between physical experience and psychological knowledge. In other words, experiencing is *additional to* reasoning and reflection (Harel and Papert 1991).

In their 2005 paper, Bürgi, Jacobs and Roos take this a step further and propose that getting 'hands on' actually helps the brain directly through *physiological* processes. They quote Wilson (1998), because of his leadership in the field of 'hand' research: 'any theory of human intelligence which ignores the interdependence of hand and brain function . . . is grossly misleading,' and – 'we make movements with our hands to help us think' (McGinnis 2002).

Among the heavyweight strategy academics, Mintzberg (1987) described the strategist as a potter and craftswoman. Using this metaphor, which has become a memorable classic, Mintzberg described how the potter senses the possibilities of the clay (strategy) with her hands. While crafting the pot she is interacting with this substance (that she understands intimately), working it physically into shapes that she is simultaneously imagining in her mind. In this way, the pot emerges to be what it is, the outcome of experience, competence and practice, as well as intentional design.

Lewis' experience

I think this is a very natural process. To children, the world seems over-whelmingly complex and too full of too much information. To cope with this we develop skills for recognising pattern and structure, we identify the significant patterns and ignore the rest. We have skills for forcing the patterns into different ones by experimenting, exploring and playing. This is how we learn, by repeating loops of trials and tests. This is learning from first principles. This is hard work, the constant search for new data and information, learning and adapting according to what we find. Unfortunately as we grow up we get lazier and discard these learning principles and live with the template of the resulting pattern, forgetting how the templates came about.

One of the most important realisations for children is that other people have their own lives, make their own decisions and don't always do this in predictable ways. Children live a life of anxiety, anticipating what others will do. Because children are anxious for order; they want to find patterns and they will do almost anything to get there, they are fearless explorers and uninhibited in their search for knowledge.

As adults we tend to live in more constrained worlds, we tend to do more predictable, acceptable things around each other. We are supposed to show-up wearing clothes, speak the same language, and so we make assumptions, we get lazy and these assumptions are made on what worked in the past, for old patterns. Adults need to be more like children if they are going to find new patterns and new strategies.

The brain and hands are very tightly linked. Manipulation of our hands assumes a lot of our brain space and energy in quite a literal sense. When modelling something – especially with two hands – and telling a story about it at the same time, the brain is suffused with blood and neural activity is stimulated – there is a huge amount of brain activity. People feel more tired after a day modelling than spending a day in conversation. It seems there is something innate in us about using our hands and building models. Better yet is to do this in a playful manner and go back to the childhood skills of exploring for new patterns and knowledge.

Playing imaginatively

In terms of the strategy process, first there is sense-making and then there is imagination, ideas and creative solutions.

Some theory

Imagination is fundamental to the idea of playing. According to Roos and Victor (1999) there are three types of imagination involved in serious play and which constitute strategic imagination: the imagination to describe what is going on and see possibilities, the imagination to create completely new possibilities and the imagination to challenge the status quo and start afresh.

Descriptive imagination

This is the process of making sense of our experience and of finding ways to describe 'the way of the world'.

In strategy, there are numerous tools and models that help us to frame the 'where are we now' understanding of our business or industry. The Five Forces model, the Directional Policy Matrix, Value Chains, 2-by-2 matrix models, 3-circle diagrams and scenario stories help organise information about the competitive landscape, categorise customers, set boundaries about choices and decisions or rehearse possible futures to find new directions. These describe our experience and knowledge; they tap into our technical competence and judgement. These models are constructed because we believe that when used 'cleverly' they can help provide insights into what to do next, where the profitable gaps are that can be filled, how recombinations or realignments might create new value. None of these represent the full and accurate reality of the business, industry or domain. They are theoretical, conceptual, abstract descriptions that traditionally are represented in 2D format.

Changing the medium to 3D and tapping into our human and naturally superior way to make descriptions of the here-and-now raise the quality of this type of imagination.

Creative imagination

Roos and Victor (1999) define this as what we often mistake for imagination itself. Creativity is the discovery of what could be. It is the light-bulb moment when we discover what is missing, what is just waiting to be – it is the new-to-the-world idea.

Vision, inspiration, foresight and insight are craved for in the business world. How to get this spark of genius or find the creative solution is harder to prescribe. The traditional strategic methods of analysis, review, deeper investigation of the data, an external perspective and so on are commonly practised but rarely result in great new ideas.

So, how might play help this type of imagination?

Players in games appear to 'lose themselves' and get into the 'flow' where they are capable of 'high levels' of brain functioning. According to researchers at the LEGO® Learning Institute (2011) this is one of the four qualities of mind that are critical to play – the ability to focus and to experience 'flow'. Flow is described as 'an optimal experience where our abilities are in balance with the challenges at hand'.

Another of these four qualities is 'rule breaking'. In the words of the LEGO® Learning Institute: 'adopting a beginner's mindset enables us to explore ideas further, unconstrained by what we already know'.

Challenging imagination

A metaphor for this type of imagination is the 'blank sheet of paper' approach. This describes an imagination that starts again, deconstructing the knowledge structures that have been built and beginning afresh. Researchers suggest that sarcasm and disdain for current practice or the predominant paradigm (Kuhn 1962) are the drivers for engaging this type of imagination.

Playful engagement helps the challenging imagination. Another quality of mind that is vital to sustained play is *'provocation'*. This is the ability to disrupt what we already know and allows us to stray into new areas and advance into new possibilities (LEGO® Learning Institute 2011).

Three of the four qualities of mind essential for play – flow, rule-breaking and provocation – are included above, the fourth is *mastery*. This is described as: *Caring that things are done well involves actively pursuing mastery over a medium.* This reinforces the serious nature of play in the context of strategy. It suggests that those engaged need to care and endeavour to excel at the art of being strategic.

Lewis' experience

When the team model is built, we can ask the group to act out different scenarios into the landscape. Like 'what happens if these two competitors merge?', 'what happens if this leader is poached by a competitor?', 'what happens if this technology comes into play here?' When the group acts these scenarios out, it is crystal clear if the strategy is flimsy or resilient.

I did a modelling exercise with a well-known High Street retailer. As part of their strategy, the company wanted to build the store of the future. The first model that was built was a physical store, but it was a pretty uninteresting model. It was clunky and when bricks were removed for one reason or another, it became unstable. By the end of the session we had a much more fluid idea of the relationship between the customer and the brand. The store had disappeared and what people building the model had constructed was their dream of how they would like to interact with the customer. The outcome was a new Customer Relationshiop Model (CRM) system, relationships and behaviours, not a new store. The model was a powerful voice for the people modelling. Without the bricks, we would not have found anything as exciting and imaginative.

Playing without constraint

Some theory

Perhaps the main hurdle managers and leaders have to overcome before using play techniques at work is the seeming contradiction of the two – work and play. For most of us, these activities are for different settings and different reasons. What is done at work can be defined as *telic* activity, describing its goal orientation and targeted prescription of getting things done. Compare this with the aimless (*autotelic*) activities involved in play, and work and play feel at odds with each other. Also, without a goal or intention, what value is gained from the activity? Yet, if intention or goal-pursuance is included, the exercise ceases to be playful.

Pelligrini (2009) argues that removing the constraint of an objective or goal, essentially pursuing a 'blue sky' process of exploration, testing out new arrangements of ideas and rehearsing new behaviours are fundamental to innovative behaviour and developing problem-solving capabilities. Statler et al. (2009) propose that value is likely to emerge but not from the activity directly.[3] In other words and borrowing from the popular phrase 'It is not the winning or losing, but the taking part' where the value in playing lies. So that:

- an autotelic approach acknowledges from the outset that the outcome of the exercise is unknown – there is no 'one' right answer – and that more than one possible future or solution exists. Hence, more strategic options are likely to emerge.
- this is beneficial when solving complex strategic problems and in an uncertain world. Here, exploring, testing, even making tentative investments in several options is less risky and more likely to deliver success. Kay (2010) argues compellingly for obliquity, that is pursuing objectives *indirectly*.
- also, with greater knowledge about strategic possibilities dispersed among the players involved in autotelic activity, this could result in greater preparedness for future changes in context. Statler et al. (2009) suggest that this could be defined as something akin to organisational wisdom.
- multi-level learning (social, emotional, cognitive) is an outcome of autotelic behaviour and is positively linked with gaining and sustaining competitive advantage (Senge 1990).
- autotelic activity can help individuals imagine themselves, their organisations and themselves *in* their organisations, in new ways, and this could result in different perceptions about culture and identity, enabling the possibility of fundamental organisational change (Statler et al. 2009).

Lewis' experience

If you think about strategy as purpose or identity for an organisation, modelling is really powerful as a means to discover who you are.

I was working with modelling and a large multinational manufacturer helping them resolve a complex issue with a new product and how/where to build the factory needed for its future development. The model construction became a powerful community builder and helped to ease a number of the trickier issues, from union concerns about re-purposed jobs to local authority estate licences and permissions.

In the end, it was this combination of use of the model for solution-finding and wider community bonding that opened the door to the more abstract identity, team and competitive landscape building exercises. It emerged that even as the manufacturing division finalised their plans for the new factory, the parent company decided to hive-off the unit, making it a wholly owned subsidiary which could sell its skills and projects to other industries, even to competitors of the parent group. For thousands of employees within the division, this was a crisis of identity in its sharpest form.

Both the newly constituted board of the company and two teams of its mid-level managers were set up for identity-building sessions. In facilitating for the CEO and board, I discovered a challenge at the outset was that at least two other members of the board thought they would have become the new unit's CEO. An extraordinarily rich array of metaphors was put into play, from lifeboats setting sail to new competitive horizons to legless workers representing a deep sense of comparative powerlessness. In the end, the new CEO was pleased and surprised that his colleagues had long since got over being passed over, and were already coming to the table, in best professional form, with ideas how to support him; what had been unexpressed in words and weeks of tense pre-meetings came out fluidly and productively in the narration of the board members' models. The mid-level managers, meanwhile, were able to build out some excitement around the possibilities the move might have for them.

More generically, finding identity allows you to ask lots of strategic questions: 'If this is us, why do we choose to work with this partner, or that one?', 'Why are we investing resources here?', 'Why are we thinking of selling this when it is core to who we are?' Strategy conversations are easier to have from a sound understanding of identity. Or, you might have a mess because you don't have an identity and therefore strategic decisions are hard to make.

Whatever you are doing strategically, thinking intentionally or about the future, or about customers, suppliers, competitors, modelling it will bring a richer, deeper understanding and a faster, better outcome.

Let's play

Serious play is a process that shares complexity principles and is brilliantly suited to the complex world that is our reality today. It is a process that lifts the human imagination and democratises involvement. It shortens times to getting strategic resolution and eases implementation. In summary:

   (i) 3D physical models of the strategic problem are built by stakeholders who have relevant knowledge and experience.
  (ii) Individuals tell stories about their models attributing them metaphorical meaning before negotiating their place in the bigger picture aside other stakeholder views. The process gives those involved courage to speak openly and honestly.
 (iii) 3D representations of reality are superior to the more abstract 2D concepts strategists use traditionally; the complexity that can be built into a 3D model appears to demystify strategy and increase clarity over simplified traditional conceptual models.
  (iv) This is described as a craft-type process rather than a purely analytic or reasoned approach; hands literally help the brain to think.
   (v) The process engages psychologically, physiologically and emotionally and hence gives a richer and deeper understanding of the organisation and the strategic landscape and promotes learning at many levels.
  (vi) It promotes collaboration across hierarchies; integration of what we collectively know; willingness to break the rules and think widely; memorable strategy experiences.
 (vii) It can deliver many and more imaginative and innovative strategic ideas faster and that have a greater chance of being implemented when compared with more traditional techniques.
(viii) It can help organisations re-imagine their culture and identities and thus enables fundamental change.

With so much to offer, the reason serious play is often not given strategic air-time might be all in the name and the medium?

Notes

1. Box is an innovation research, partnering and transformation consultancy founded at the London School of Economics. Lewis is an MIT graduate, Juris Doctor, Fulbright Scholar and NASA Space Grant Fellow.
2. At the age of nine, I was selected for a class that was taught mathematics using a new hands-on technique. We were given a series of wooden blocks. Some were small cubes, very similar in size to sugar cubes – the basic unit. Several of these joined together were called longs. More than two 'longs' joined with each other along their 'long sides' were called 'flats'. And 'flats' stacked on top of each other were called 'cubes'. By playing with these in a directed and deliberate way, we learnt the rules of bases (binary, denary, etc.), and of the power function and ultimately the fundamentals of logarithms – which then seemed easy. I have never forgotten it.
3. In terms of adding value, winning is not a goal that counts in play, because winning implies there is a loser and hence it is a zero-sum game.

References

Bürgi, P.T. and Roos, J. (2003). Images of Strategy. *European Management Journal* 21(1): 69–78.

Harel, I. and Papert, S. (Eds). (1991). *Constructionism*, Norwood, NJ: Ablex.

Jacobides, M.G. (2010). Strategy Tools for a Shifting Landscape. *Harvard Business Review* 88(1): 76–84.

Kay, J. (2010). Obliquity, Why Our Goals are Best Achieved Indirectly, London: Profile Books.

Kuhn, T. (1962). *The Structure of Scientific Revolutions*, Chicago: University of Chicago Press.

LEGO® Learning Institute (2011). *The Future of Play, Defining the Role and Value of Play in the Twenty First Century.* Available at: http://www.Lego.com [Accessed January 23, 2012].

McGinnis, M. (2002). How the Gesture Summons the Word. *Columbia Magazine* (Spring): 40–43. Available at: http://www.columbia.edu/cu/alumni/ Magazine/Spring2002/Krauss.html.

Mintzberg, H. (1987). Crafting Strategy. *Harvard Business Review* 65(4): 66–75.

Pelligrini, A.D. (2009). *The Role of Play in Human Development*, Oxford: Oxford University Press.

Piaget, J. (1971). *Biology and Knowledge*, Chicago: University of Chicago Press.

Pinault, L. (2004). *The Play Zone: Unlock Your Creative Genius and Connect with Customers*, New York: Harper Collins.

Plato (1991). *The Republic of Plato* (A.D Bloom trans.) 2nd ed., New York: Basic Books.

Roos, J. and Victor, B. (1999). Toward a New Model of Strategy-making as Serious Play. *European Management Journal* 17(4): 348–355.

Roos, J., Victor, B. and Statler, M. (2004). Playing Seriously with Strategy. *Long Range Planning* 37: 549–568.

Schön, D. (1963). *Displacement of Concepts*, New York: Humanities Press.

Schön, D. (1993). 'Generative Metaphor: A Perspective on Problem-setting in Social Policy', in Ortony, A. (ed), *Metaphor and Thought*, pp. 137–163, Cambridge: Cambridge University Press.

Senge, P. (1990). *The Fifth Discipline: The Art and Practice of the Learning Organisation*, London: Random House.

Snowden, D. (2005). *Simple but not Simplistic: The Art and Science of Story*. Available at: http://www.cynefin.net [Accessed August 24, 2010].

Statler, M., Roos, J. and Victor, B. (2002) *'Ain't Misbehavin': Taking Play Seriously in Organizations,'* Working Paper 17, the Imagination Lab Foundation. Available at: http://www.imagilab.org [Accessed November 14, 11].

Statler, M., Roos, J. and Victor, B. (2009). 'Ain't Misbehavin': Taking Play Seriously in Organizations'. *Journal of Change Management* 9(1): 87–107.

Von Ghyczy, T. (2003). The Fruitful Flaws of Strategy Metaphors. *Harvard Business Review* 81(9): 86–94.

Wilson, F. (1998). *The Hand: How its Use Shapes the Brain, Language, and Human Culture*, New York: Pantheon.

10
Strategy as Social Process

Bill Critchley

Introduction

The concept of strategy influences, either implicitly or explicitly, much management thinking and practice, and it tends to be informed by a particular view of what an organisation *is*. How this view is understood and applied has important implications for how we make sense of our experience as leaders and facilitators of strategic change.

The purpose of this chapter is to examine this perspective, which prevails as the current orthodoxy, and to propose a radical alternative which has significant implications for the conceptualisation and practice of strategy. The alternative offers a perspective which sees organisations as 'complex social processes' (Stacey et al., 2000), and is radical in the sense that it challenges most of the core assumptions inherent in the orthodox way of thinking about organisations.

The origins of the current orthodoxy

A key shift in the evolution of organisation in the early 1800s was the emergence of non-owner 'managers' when managers tended to be seen as the masters and oppressors of working people. The shift was driven in part by the desire of this emerging managerial class to gain the same legitimacy as that enjoyed by lawyers and physicians.

The way of gaining professional respectability in those times was to hitch one's wagon to the enlightenment project by making claims to rational and objective scientific rigour. The desire to claim scientific legitimacy was primarily driven by the need of managers for identity, established through power and status, which began, from around the late 1800s in the USA, to be conferred on managers through the acquisition of an MBA, the passport to managerial position and privilege.

Then in 1911, Frederick Winslow Taylor, normally seen along with Henri Fayol as one of the 'founding fathers of "scientific management"', published his book, *The Principles of Scientific Management* (Taylor, 1911), and in 1917 Fayol published *Administration Industrielle et Générale* (Fayol, 1917).

Taylor's interest was the observation and analysis of the components of a job, and the identification of the skills needed to perform the job. Fayol's interest was similar; he proposed there were five primary functions of management and 14 principles, the first mentioned being the division of work – he focused on splitting an organisation into a number of specialist activities, and consequently job analysis, time and motion and organisation design were the main legacies of Taylor and Fayol.

These two powerful voices established management as a rational, 'scientific' set of activities, consisting in forecasting, planning, organising, controlling and coordinating, with the corollary that organisations exist as units in an economic system that can be manipulated to maximise efficiency. The principle assumptions underpinning this conception of organisations and management were that efficient causality could be established, and rules could be set which workers would follow. This casts workers as rule-following 'agents'. Indeed Taylor recommended that managers hire men, sound in body but not burdened with any desire or capacity to think, which would potentially obstruct the rational direction and control of the managerial elite!

It would seem that any considerations about the ethical implications of depriving the majority of the work force of any self-determination were, and still are in many contemporary organisations, largely ignored. Perhaps that is why we are experiencing around the world an increasing number of broadly anti-capitalist protests, with bankers tending to bear the brunt of some fairly inchoate expression of anger against a social order that seems to bestow wealth and privilege on a tiny minority at the expense of the majority.

One of the major problems inherent in this 'scientific' perspective is that human beings will not slavishly follow rules. This has always been true, although at the dawn of the industrial revolution people were more willing to trade autonomy for the promise of material well-being. With the contemporary shift to the 'knowledge economy', and its requirement for creative talent, it becomes even more obvious that the mechanistic conception of management simply cannot work in the long run.

Recognising this new reality still seems too heretical for many managers schooled into the belief of the management prerogative, although the economic debacle of 2008 should have provided some of the most convincing evidence to disturb this mind-set.

Current approaches to strategy

These twin pillars of orthodox management thinking, efficient causality and scientific psychology, have formed the bedrock of most Western 'Business School' teaching until this day, and still constitute the dominant managerial discourse, and this of course includes thinking about strategy.

The school of strategic thinking which has had most influence in business can be described as the school of 'strategic choice' – a transformational process in which organisations adapt to environmental changes by restructuring themselves in an intentional, rational manner. There have been a number of writers broadly within the school of 'strategic choice', and the one who is probably most familiar to managers is Michael Porter (Porter, 1980). He suggested that leaders had three main types of choice: 'cost leadership' strategy, a 'differentiation' strategy or a 'focus' strategy.

There is a generic methodology that is implied by the notion of 'strategic choice' which is generally followed by all writers, and is quite familiar to most managers, so a brief overview will serve. The methodology breaks down into four main phases. The first is to carry out some industry analysis, to understand the structure and market dynamics of the industry in which the company operates, and to identify trends, opportunities and threats. The next phase is to carry out an analysis of the business's current position in the market in relation to its main competitors (competitive analysis, share and profitability analysis and so forth) and to undertake a diagnosis of the organisation's strengths and weaknesses. The third phase consists in identifying strategic options, and the final phase is concerned with making and implementing a strategic *choice*.

Most senior managers, and anyone who has been to business school with their emphasis on rational analysis, will recognise what is essentially a process of *aligning* the company to its environment. We are familiar with it and it appears to have some face validity, so we probably have not thought to question this established and habitual way of approaching business strategy.

However, if we closely examine some of the assumptions which inform the school of strategic choice, many of them appear to have become, at best, obsolete, and quite probably wrong.

The first assumption is that environmental changes are largely identifiable and that future states can by and large be predicted. We now realise that we live in a highly unpredictable world, and this has become almost a truism. When some scientists in the US defence establishment developed a way of exchanging research information via a 'web', no one could have forecasted what impact this development would have on the way we live our lives; even when the Internet was established in its early days, its effects were wildly exaggerated and underestimated at the same time. So the idea that managers can predict future states and base plans upon them does not resonate with experience.

Furthermore, while one firm is working out its strategy, so are all its competitors, either formally or informally. As each player *acts* into its competitive landscape, so it changes it, and as all competitors in a market are simultaneously acting into the 'market' landscape, it is clear that the combined impact is complex and dynamic. Taking this one step further, I would suggest that a 'market' as such is a metaphor or a convenient linguistic construction. The 'market' does not exist independently of the businesses and the consumers who create it. We are all participants in a process of interaction, affecting it and being affected by it at the same time. When you think about it, this seems common sense, but we have developed a habit of *thought* which speaks of 'the market' as a set of impersonal forces having an independent existence outside of the companies who compete with each other. This is clearly nonsense. We are all 'participants' in the 'market' creating it by the decisions we make and being created by it *at the same time.* Clearly an asset manager acting on behalf of a large insurance company has much more influence than a single individual, but it is nevertheless the on-going interactions between people which create the 'market'.

This realisation – that we are affecting and being affected by our environment *at the same time* – calls into question another assumption of the strategic choice school, that of clear cut cause-and-effect links, where one thing affects another in a clearly defined linear fashion. Most managers are familiar with the experience of unintended consequences, but these are usually seen as the result of poor planning or poor implementation.

The Emperor has no clothes

Increasingly, managers are finding that the conventional nostrums of management theory do not explain their lived experience of unpredictability, complexity and lack of control. On the whole they tend to assume that this is either because they are not applying them properly, or it is because they do not know all they are supposed to know – someone out there has a solution. However when theory does not explain experience, the sensible thing to do is to develop a better theory, and this is what 'complexity theory', or a version adapted to the social nature of organisations, offers.

The core premise of the theory of 'complex social processes' is that organisations *consist in* on-going processes of dynamic interaction, of continually emerging understandings and responses and reconfiguring of priorities and activities. This is a different onotology which sees organisation as *process* rather than as entity. Thus an organisation has no materiality or substance, but it is continuously emerging through the communicative interactions of people as they go on together. Acknowledging this newly understood 'truth' leads to the realisation that managers may be in charge, but they are not in control in the long run (Streatfield, 2001). Reg Revans (Revans, 1980) made the distinction between 'programmed knowledge', when a manager is faced with a 'puzzle', and complex problems. Short run, operational puzzles, such as how to optimise a manufacturing process, may give the illusion of control, but most of what managers face, particularly in the realm of 'strategy', are long run, complex organisational problems. The best a manager can do is to pay attention to emerging phenomena and continuously respond and adapt.

The complexity perspective

The contribution of complexity science

The early formulations of complexity theory were radical in that they proposed a new way to make sense of phenomena in the world, a way that shocked the scientific community when the first inklings of it began to emerge in the early part of the last century. It proposed that order emerges out of chaos without any external design agency. As Stuart Kauffman (Kauffman, 1996) puts it, 'Order emerges for free'. Such a way of seeing inevitably has major implications for society, religion, politics and, of course, organisations. If no external design agency is required for order to emerge, then what is the role of the manager in organisations?

What was discovered was a new kind of order; it was not predictable, repeatable, reproducible order, but unpredictable *pattern*, pattern which cannot be foretold from the original conditions. There seemed to be a principle of *self-organisation* at work. There are many examples of this in nature, for example swans flocking, termites building complex structures and so forth. Through the development of computer simulations scientists similarly discovered self-organised, emergent order. The simulations consisted of a number of simple programmes or 'agents', each agent being given some rules of interaction about what to do when it encountered another agent. The important point here is that *there was no overall blueprint for how the simulation would unfold* – all that was given were rules of interaction to each individual agent.

The key discovery was that as the simulation was set in motion, and the agents interacted with each other, a *pattern* emerged which could not have been predicted from the *local* rules of interaction. With simple rules of interaction, only one type of pattern emerged; but with more complex rules, including rules for replication, patterns generated further patterns and the agents modified the rules of interaction – *as if the agents had learned to adapt themselves to their environment and adapt their environment at the same time*. Once again none of this was predetermined or prescribed. A further characteristic of these patterns was that they were not uniform, or to put it another way they were similar and different at the same time. Order emerges in the form of patterns, and these patterns are stable and unstable at the same time, because the on-going processes of agents interacting in complex ways produce stability *and* change *at the same time*.

So, four important characteristics emerged from the complexity simulations which would seem to have some face validity for organisations, namely *self-organisation, emergence, pattern,* and *stability/instability at the same time*.

The challenge to current thinking

Managerial language is full of control metaphors – we talk of 'driving the change agenda', of 'managing change' and of finding the point of 'maximum leverage' in the 'system' to bring about change. To really understand the implications of the complexity perspective is to recognise that such language is meaningless and obsolete. Yet many of the books and articles on the subject written by management theorists are still shot through with these sorts of phrases.

Order in the universe cannot be predicted or made to happen. At the same time, we are all familiar with recurrent patterns in organisations which seem to occur under certain conditions. This tempts us to believe that if we can understand the cause of these patterns, we can also understand how to create new patterns. This misunderstands the core insight of the complexity perspective made earlier, which is that by their complex and dynamic nature social processes are inherently unpredictable and uncontrollable.

If we attend carefully to the language of some organisation theorists who have encountered complexity theory and seek to 'apply it' to organisations, it reveals their underlying assumptions. For example, some talk about how to 'move' an organisation from one 'attractor' to a more desirable one (an attractor being a concept drawn from quantum physics to describe the apparent focal point of a dynamic system). Others, who have come across the early work with computerised simulations which used only a few simple rules, talk of identifying the few rules which will lead to a desirable new pattern.

The mistake such writers make is to take the results of some experiments undertaken under controlled scientific conditions and extrapolate them to social conditions. It is but a short step to a new set of toolkits and recipes, wrapped up in pseudo scientific terminology, on how to 'manage' complexity. And we are back full circle to the sometimes banal and often grandiose managerialist language of individual control, unitary purpose, and cause and effect.

The development of complexity thinking in relation to organisations

Stacey et al. (2000) developed the theory of 'complex social processes' which is a synthesis of sociology, psychology and some insights from complexity theory which do seem to shed some light on the nature of organisations. But it is rooted in sociology and the work of George Mead (Mead, 1934) and Norbert Elias (Elias and Kilminster, 1991). The core premise is that organisations consist of human beings in an on-going process of communicative interaction, affecting and being affected by their environment, but not in control over it or each other. The temptation is to think, because human beings *employ* artefacts (buildings, machines, etc.) and *create* artefacts (products, logos, patents,etc,), that these artefacts constitute the organisation. What I am arguing is that when we talk about an organisation we are actually referring to a process of organising which itself consists in communicative interaction.

The 'organisation' *emerges* in the various patterns and flows of communication as people go on together. The term 'organisation' is a 'social construction'; it is a mental construct created in the meanings people make together, some formalised in brands, logos, contracts of employment, and some negotiated in the informal conversations which are the stuff of organisational life. It is not held by any one individual but is constantly being re-created through the conversations and interactions that people experience together. A sense of organisational identity develops over time through the norms and habits, the stories and myths, the historical recollections and shared history; it is *social* through and through, and it is continuously being renegotiated in a never-ending process of communicative interaction which manifests as the meetings, reports, policies, procedures, structures and such that people experience as the 'stuff of organisational life'. This is a *process* view of organisation which argues that an organisation, unlike natural phenomena, has no *essential qualities*, nothing that makes it an object in its own right worthy of a noun 'organisation' to describe it. The members of the (processes of) organisation are *participants* in creating a social process which continuously evolves into an unknown future. We cannot by definition get outside it; as participants we simultaneously create and are created by the process of engaging together in joint action.

Mead described this process of communicative interaction rather succinctly. He said; 'The meaning of the gesture is in the response.' He used the word 'gesture' to mean any communicative move, verbal or physical, towards another. While as humans we gesture with intention – for example, I want to convey some information to you, ask you to do something, scare you, convince you or whatever – it is only in your response that the 'meaning' of the interaction emerges. Imagine that I move to shake your hand at the end of a quarrel, but you respond to it as an aggressive gesture and move away, and I run after you…so in a series of gestures and responses, patterns of meaning emerge. This is a spontaneous dance of meaning making in which neither party can predict the other's response. They can anticipate but not predict, and in a conversation of gestures during which each party is well attuned to the other, the gesturer will be modifying her gesture even as she gestures and notices the respondent's shift in expression, or body posture.

This notion challenges the traditional way of thinking about communication as the transfer of information from one brain to another (rather like digital data is copied from one computer to another), and instead sees communication as a dynamic and non-linear process whereby meaning arises in the process of interaction, being negotiated and constructed in a way that enables the possibility of novelty, or 'learning' to emerge.

Patterns of gesture and response are of course mediated by cultural norms and language rules which enable shared meaning to be more or less arrived at quite quickly; but in a complex exchange, misunderstandings and different interpretations are the norm rather than the exception. In organisations, rules about how things are to be done, custom and practice, and organisational norms fulfil a similar stabilising effect, but we begin to understand that this emergent process of communicative interaction is inherently unpredictable and hence uncontrollable in the way that scientific management and systems theorists have assumed. Much conventional management theory speaks of the need for alignment, but contrary to this received wisdom, it is through misunderstanding, contention and a certain amount of messiness that novelty (and hence innovation) emerges. This has major implications for the way leaders and consultants think about the nature of organisational strategy.

The complexity perspective challenges managers to act in the knowledge that they have no control, only influence. They can advocate and aspire, but they cannot predict. There are no absolute truths, only ethical decisions to be made in the here and now. This may be a difficult premise to accept at first because it runs so counter to our habits of thought, but it begins to appeal to common sense.

Indeed I introduced this perspective to a leading professional services firm, who had brought in a head of strategy to bring a greater sense of shared direction and coordinated implementation into their business. They were having difficulty embedding a formal and systematic strategic approach in their networked, knowledge-based, partnership type of organisation. The complexity perspective resonated with their experience and helped them make sense of why 'strategic planning' was simply not working.

One of the real difficulties for us as managers is that while we have no absolute control in the long run, and we cannot predict with any certainty the outcomes of our actions, we remain responsible for them. It behoves us to pay attention to the impacts and effects of our decisions and to reflect thoughtfully on our intentions, and in the light of experience to attempt to anticipate their likely consequences, and to enter again into the never ending cycle of action, enquiry, reflection, action and so on.

Implications for managers

We have all had the experience of attending regular meetings, where there is a fixed agenda and the participants are usually the same. Often the meeting takes place in the same room at the same time, but while there is a familiar *pattern*, the meetings are never exactly the same – different conversations, slightly different combinations of people and so on. So our experience confirms how conversational patterns emerge in organisational life, some of them formal (such as the meeting's agenda and topics of discussion) and some of them informal (such as the sense-making that takes place outside of the formal topics, the 'gossip' or rumour).

We have experience of how a key event, such as a heated exchange, a particular decision, the inclusion or exclusion of an individual can shift the pattern of interaction, either temporarily or permanently. We have the experience of being taken by surprise, of not anticipating that a particular event would lead to a particular outcome. So our experience tells us that change is unpredictable, that small differences can amplify into larger pattern shifts.

We also know that managerial practice consists in engaging in myriads of connecting meetings and conversations through which we attempt to negotiate and agree joint action. Purposive 'joint action' is broadly what organisations are formed for, and it is continually being negotiated. We know that power differentials play a part in these negotiations, and that what emerges is rarely entirely predictable, and by no means rational, and yet, because we are steeped in the conventions and assumptions of scientific and systemic management, we continue to believe we can plan and control change! Complexity theory confirms what we learn from our experience, but what our education and conditioning makes it hard for us to accept.

What I have described above in referring to 'myriads of connecting meetings and conversations' is what I see as the main *currency* of organisations. Much of this is informal in nature, but clearly organisations require good enough, minimalist structures to manage short-term performance, sensible procedures for managing work flows, good systems for managing performance and money and so on. This is the stuff of ordinary management with which all managers are very familiar; it is clearly important to do it well, but because of the influence of machine thinking it is often overdone.

Particularly in organisations with a bureaucratic history, the capacity for self-organisation is largely suppressed, so that all change is seen to need elaborate planning and the development of detailed blueprints before anything can happen. This focus on getting the 'right structure' is often not only painfully slow, it can also have the opposite effect to that which was intended, or at best reproduce what is already present (such as re-structuring an organisation without attending to how members relate or how they do what they do).

Implications for strategy

It is helpful for managers to think of themselves as in charge but not in control. This requires them to act with intention by formulating strategic intentions (*anticipating* possible outcomes) in the knowledge that they cannot predict outcome.

Strategy, as my good friend Patricia Shaw (Shaw, 2002) observed, is the interaction between chance and intention, so what they need to do, having formulated a strategic intention, is to work with and learn from the outcomes which *actually* emerge, rather than spend precious time in analysing 'what went wrong'. So this suggests two core strategic activities: *formulating intentions* and *responding* to consequences.

A case study

When working for Ashridge Consulting, a colleague and I were invited by a division of a reasonably large engineering group to help them with their 'strategy'.

Each 'business' within the group had its own infrastructure, in particular its own sales force, and quite understandably staff saw this site as the source of their livelihood, and the sales people strove to win orders for it, often in competition with other members of the same Group.

An emerging group of powerful global customers now sought a more integrated response, expressed in the jargon of the day as a requirement to be a 'global player', a 'virtual company', particularly in the areas of price, quality and service. These customers were threatening to withdraw their business unless this supplier 'got its act together'.

Our first contact

We were invited to attend a meeting of the 'change group', which was effectively the Board with one or two additional people, as observers so that we would learn something about the business and the key players.

At some point I was asked whether I had any observations, and I made some comments about the process, particularly the way, as it seemed to me, the Chief Executive (CE) had, in a chairman-like way, ridden over any disagreements or contentious areas. He took this to heart, more than I had expected, and frequently referred to it throughout the assignment, with good humour, but in a manner which suggested it had been a significant moment to him. It did seem to be a defining moment in that it established in their minds what sort of consultants we were and what sort of relationship we were going to have. This was despite the fact that my colleague, who is a powerful character, made some extremely perceptive points about the business issues they were facing, which they took little notice of. Thus the leadership of the assignment informally fell to me through my *direct participation* in the *communicative patterns*.

The process which evolved

The change group had identified a number of strategic issues that they thought needed addressing, and their plan was to nominate some staff to task groups, bring them all together at a conference and 'set them off' so to speak. They wanted us to design and manage this for them, and then 'train' the groups in how to lead strategic change, and get 'buy in'. We argued that their model of strategic change, whereby they identified the strategic issues and assigned people to tasks, would neither ensure that they were addressing the most important issues nor that anyone would 'buy in'.

We persuaded them that a process whereby a large group of managers met over two days to identify the issues, and organise themselves around those issues, would be more likely to create 'buy in', and stimulate the organisation's innovative capability. This idea was strongly resisted by some members of the Board who saw it as usurping their 'right' to decide what the issues were, and it challenged their assumption that their view would be the 'right' view. However it seemed to resonate with the CE's experience of the limitations of the usual 'top–down' approach to the formulation of strategic intention.

We started with a two-day workshop for about 50 managers to begin a dialogue about what becoming 'global' would entail. We had two process intentions in mind; one was for the CE to express his general intention without being too specific about the 'how', and the other was to expand and deepen the quality of communicative interaction through creating opportunities for people to start talking and addressing problems in groupings that crossed their normal country, site or national boundaries.

Our longer-term intention was to challenge the boundaries of their thinking, and to provoke them into experimentation with innovative ways of working. For example, as engineers they tended to tackle problems with 'project groups', with defined terms of reference, a clear statement of goals, milestones and methodologies. This was very much part of their existing culture or pattern, and while it solved problems incrementally, it was unlikely to create any innovative strategies.

The workshop was a new experience for most participants, and by their standards it was quite messy. On the first day we had some well thought through design, to introduce people to the 'global' intention, and identify the issues that this gave rise to. We asked Board members to participate in the group discussions, and from time to time to take up their role as the Board, and sit in the middle of the room, responding in real time to these issues as they came up. Some members of the Board were very uncomfortable with this, but for most participants it symbolised something totally different and welcome in terms of management style, and the only question was whether it would be sustained. On the second day we designed on the hoof, in order to get to a manageable number of issues and to have some people taking ownership of these issues.

The change initiative groups

Five change initiatives formed, and we subsequently worked with each one to help them define what was *really* important in the broad area they had chosen, what could usefully be a project, and how to tackle what could not be turned into a project.

Some six months later we brought these groups together with the Board to review their activities, to learn together and to develop further initiatives. This was the process designed to learn and *respond* to the consequences of enacting the strategic intention.

Commentary

This example highlights, in my view, the importance of maintaining both stability (providing a clear intention and a process structure), and creative instability in the process of working strategically. On the boundary between stability and instability, so the theory goes, lies the possibility of optimum creativity. In organisational terms this means working on the boundary between the formal and the informal, and this is one of the ideas which informed the overall design of our work.

We started with a reasonably large grouping, which we kept working in one large room (we did not have break-out rooms) in order for people to have a better sense of themselves in a wider context, thereby stimulating connectivity. Within some broad parameters we invited them to explore their reality, to discover what the issues were, as opposed to giving them a diagnosis and asking them to work on the problems (the approach which was first mooted by the client), and we allowed groups to form around the issues which emerged rather than attempt to assign individuals to issues (self-organisation).

It is interesting to observe that senior managers did not think that the 'right' issues had been identified, but we encouraged them to let this rather messy process of self-organisation unfold rather than have them impose their own change agenda, and many of the groups subsequently redefined the issue they were working on, thereby demonstrating their capacity for creative self-regulation.

Finally we realised how important it was that senior managers did in fact join the change groups but not as the group leader. They were thus not excluded from the process as they would have been in a 'bottom–up approach', but were able to influence it by participating in the informal processes of the organisation, as opposed to exerting their influence through their formal leadership role, evoking compliant responses to the exercise of formal power, and inhibiting the organisation's potential for innovative self-organisation.

Usually, when I present this case study, I am asked what the 'results' of this strategic initiative were. This is a frustrating question when I may have just spent some time arguing that organisations are dynamic and non-linear, and hence it is impossible to make linear connections between action and effect. It is also understandable, coming, as it does from such a deeply ingrained habit of thinking in causal, linear sequences of the 'if this…then that' variety. It is such a fundamental tenet of managerial thinking that we take action 'in order to' achieve something, which it is hard to gainsay without being thought a naïve fool.

However what we achieved is what we did. We enabled a different pattern of conversation, which provoked, excited and disturbed in equal measure. The question it is reasonable to ask is that to what extent the pattern disturbance amplified around the organisation, increasing its innovative potential, and to what extent 'old' patterns reasserted themselves afterwards. I don't know the answer to this question, but I assume some of the old patterns would inevitably reassert themselves, and I hope that some 'learning' took place which would lead to new and more innovative ways of responding to emerging strategic issues.

Some practical principles

Let me conclude by suggesting some practical principles which are implied by this perspective:

- Managers are supposed to be in charge, and yet they find it difficult to stay in control. It is helpful for managers to think of themselves as in charge but not in control. This requires them to act with intention (anticipating possible outcomes) in the knowledge that they cannot predict outcome. What they need to do is to work with, and learn from the outcomes which *actually* emerge, rather than spend precious time in analysing 'what went wrong'.

- Managers need to be relieved of the expectation that they should always know what to do/be able to diagnose the problem/find the solution – these only *emerge* through engaging in processes of conversation.
- It is more important and useful for managers to turn their attention to how things actually get done (informal processes of conversation) rather than to designing systems and procedures in the belief that this is how things ought to be done.
- It is also important for managers to inquire into what works well and to encourage it.
- What sustains organisational continuity and what makes for creative change are the messy processes of social interaction.
- Systems and procedures are merely codified and routinised conversations – at best they will represent good practice in, for example, quality maintenance, safety, recruitment and so on. At worst they may become an obsolete and cumbersome set of procedures which inhibit innovation.
- Diversity is key to innovation. The pursuit of organisational harmony, consistency, shared values and total collaboration is inimical to innovation – diversity and difference, messiness and contention are necessary for creativity and transformation.
- Managers need to engage in both the formal and the informal processes, paradoxically maintaining stability/consistency and provoking novelty and innovation at the same time.
- Power differentials need to be minimised if diversity and difference and hence the possibility of novelty is to emerge.
- Change starts *locally*. It is far more effective to foster local initiatives and experiments than to embark on costly, formalised 'whole organisation' change programmes.

In summary, I suggest that organisations are complex social processes which are characterised simultaneously by stability and instability. Stable patterns of interaction tend to be maintained through designed, legitimate networks of roles and accountabilities through which people pursue official goals and policies. Instability, and hence the possibility of transformation, emerges locally in the simultaneous operation of many informal networks in which significant political, social and other processes are at work contributing in vitally important ways to the effectiveness of the organisation. In my experience the prevailing assumptions which inform much managerial behaviour and consulting practice are still mainly machine based, which leads to an over-emphasis on the importance of and need to control the legitimate system through structural, procedural and programmatic solutions.

The radical complexity perspective suggests that organisations continually emerge in an unpredictable way as they evolve into the unknown. Strategy from this perspective is merely the process whereby senior people orchestrate a conversation about future intentions and possibilities, based on their best anticipations of market opportunities, and a realistic assessment of the company's capabilities. It assumes that no group in the organisation has a monopoly of wisdom, that mobilising the collective intelligence within an organisation is more likely to come up with creative but sensible ideas than an overly engineered, linear planning process and that 'strategy', at its best, is an experimental and innovative process. There are, of course, exceptions to every rule, when single individuals or elites have for a while appeared to successfully drive a company's strategic development through the force of their personalities and particular creative vision. Our culture loves a hero and we are inclined to massage the evidence in favour of the hero myth, but it is always questionable how 'single-handed' such a process actually was. In the long run the evidence suggests that participative approaches to strategic development are more sustainable.

Strategic leadership consists in large part in mobilising the intelligence of an organisation, articulating strategic intentions and constraints, convening conversations to enquire into emerging themes and issues and supporting initiatives and experimentation.

Leaders have the paradoxical role of establishing and maintaining the necessary structure and processes through which the organisation 'manages' its everyday business, while *at the same time* provoking and stimulating the innovation which is necessary for the organisation to continuously respond, transform itself and create its future.

References

Elias, N. and Kilminster, R. (1991). *The symbol theory*, Sage: London.
Fayol, H. (1917). *Administration industrielle et générale: Prévoyance, organisation, commandement, coordination, controle*, Paris: H. Dunod et E. Pinat.

Kauffman, S.A. (1996). *At home in the universe: The search for laws of self-organization and complexity*, London: Penguin.

Mead, G.H. (1934). *Mind, self and society*, Chicago: Chicago University Press.

Porter, M.E. (1980). *Competitive strategy: Techniques for analyzing industries and competitors*, New York: Free Press.

Revans, R.W. (1980). *Action learning: New techniques for management*, London: Blond and Briggs.

Shaw, P. (2002). *Changing conversations in organizations: A complexity approach to change*, London; New York: Routledge.

Stacey, R.D., Griffin, D. and Shaw, P. (2000). *Complexity and management: Fad or radical challenge to systems thinking?* London: Routledge.

Streatfield, P.J. (2001). *The paradox of control in organizations*, London: Routledge.

Taylor, F.W. (1911). *Scientific Management*, New York: Harper.

Index